FULL
SURRENDER

J. Edwin Orr

M.A. (Northwestern)
Th. D. (Northern)
D. Phil. (Oxford)

With an Introduction by
BILLY GRAHAM

Original Publisher:
London
MARSHALL, MORGAN & SCOTT
Edinburgh

LONDON
MARSHALL, MORGAN & SCOTT, LTD.
I-5 PORTPOOL LANE,
HOLBORN, E.C.I

AUSTRALIA
317 COLLINS STREET
MELBOURNE

NEW ZEALAND
23 MONTGOMERY ROAD
ROTHESAY ROAD
AUCKLAND

SOUTH AFRICA
P.O. BOX 1720, STURK'S BUILDINGS
CAPE TOWN

CANADA
EVANGELICAL PUBLISHERS
241 YOUNG STREET
TORONTO

First published 1951
Second impression 1953
Third impression 1955
Fourth impression 1957

MADE AND PRINTED IN GREAT BRITAIN BY PURNELL AND SONS, LTD.
PAULTON (SOMERSET) AND LONDON

Republished 2017 by Enduring Word
ISBN: 978-1-939466-32-7
*Copied from the Fourth Impression
With Permission from the family of
the late Dr. J. Edwin Orr*

Resources from Dr. J. Edwin Orr may be found at:
www.jedwinorr.com

INTRODUCTION
By WILLIAM FRANKLIN GRAHAM, D.D., LL.D.

D R. J. EDWIN ORR, in my opinion, is one of the greatest authorities on the history of religious revivals in the Protestant world. I think that God has given him one of the greatest and most unique ministries anywhere in the nation, and his contribution to the Revival which I believe is on the way is invaluable. I know of no man who has a greater passion for worldwide revival or a greater love for the souls of men.

About fifteen years ago I first heard of Edwin Orr through his books. His books on faith were a tremendous blessing in my own life. Twelve years ago I met him in Florida for the first time. Thus began an acquaintance which has ripened into warm friendship.

In 1947, during our evangelistic campaigns in Great Britain, I heard that Dr. Orr was engaged in research into the nineteenth-century awakenings, so I wrote him at Oxford University and afterwards spent half a day there, viewing the sights of the ancient city and making the most of an opportunity to discuss the story of past revivals and the dreams and hopes of another in our generation.

The outstanding memory of my visit on Oxford's campus was the study-bedroom in Lincoln College where John Wesley and his young friends started the "Holy Club" with its later development into the evangelical revival of the eighteenth century. Edwin and I felt constrained to pray there for a repetition of the movements of the eighteenth and nineteenth centuries. His word on revival caused me to do a great deal of thinking which God used to bear fruit in later years.

Since 1949, in Minnesota, California, Washington and other states of the Union, Edwin Orr has been used mightily, particularly on university and college campuses. Great spiritual awakenings have followed in the wake of his ministry at Bethel College, Northern Baptist Seminary and other outstanding institutions. In late August 1949 it was my privilege to be one of the speakers at the Forrest Home College Briefing Conference in the beautiful San Bernardino Mountains of California. The messages Dr. Orr gave as one of the other speakers were of tremendous blessing in my own life. His logical development of the whole subject of full surrender and the outpouring of the Spirit stirred the entire conference, evening by evening.

During the many intervening months we have remained in close contact. Dr. Orr's work among the stars and starlets of the entertainment world is already well known, and it was through that effort that I was led of God to make contacts which later resulted in the conversion of more than one Hollywood personality.

This present volume, Dr. Orr's fifteenth book, consists of chapters based upon those talks at Forrest Home which provoked under God a real stirring among the students. I do not expect that all my Christian friends will agree with all the terminology used by the author of this book. I shall be disappointed if mere points of terminology are allowed to hide the spiritual arguments of the case which has influenced the thinking of so many. I write this introduction with the heartfelt prayer that the message of full surrender will produce much fruit in the lives of Christians who are hungry for spiritual quickening in these days.

BILLY GRAHAM

CONTENTS

SURRENDER

Forgive me, Lord, that I have failed so often,
  Striving so hard, yet striving all in vain,
Thinking to conquer self and sinful nature,
  Instead of which I taste defeat again.

Things I would do, I long leave unaccomplished;
  Things that I hate, I far too often do:
In wretchedness my heart cries for the answer
  Who shall deliver me? I wish I knew.

"Then sin some more that Grace may be the greater?"
  O Lord forbid! That cannot be the way!
Deliverance there must be found in Jesus,
  And victory for me o'er sin today.

Hast Thou a word to help me, Blessed Master,
  To show me how to run aright the race?
Or must I wander on alone in twilight
And seldom see the sunshine of Thy face?

"Confess thy sins: the Blood has power to cleanse thee;
  Submit thy will, and make it one with Mine:
Accept by faith the joy of promised blessing,
  And start afresh to walk in light divine!"

Is it so simple then—to take by trusting,
  Just as I did when I was born again?
I see it now, it's in the Cross for asking,
  And ask I will, the victory to gain.

I hunger and I thirst for Thee, Lord Jesus!
  O quench that thirst within my inmost heart:
Take all my life that I to Thee surrender,
  And may the blessing nevermore depart.

Not for myself I ask for power, Lord Jesus!
  Rather to win the souls of men to Thee,
I give myself in reasonable service—
  May I be Spirit-filled abundantly.

EDWIN ORR

CHAPTER ONE

BROKEN VOWS

WHY IS it that hundreds of well-meaning Christians attend conventions and conferences for the deepening of the spiritual life, enjoy the ministry there given, return to life's vocations with a feeling of improvement, yet speedily lapse into their former ways of backsliding and defeat? There are many reasons, but one of the least noted is the matter of incomplete consecration, the sin of broken vows. Too many Christians make a bargain with God and fail to pay their part of the price. This is sin.

A striking example of the failure of Christians to keep their word is found in the story of Ananias and Sapphira in the Acts of the Apostles narrative.

"But a man named Ananias with his wife Sapphira sold a piece of property, and with his wife's knowledge he kept back some of the proceeds, and brought only a part and laid it at the apostles' feet. But Peter said, 'Ananias, why has Satan filled your heart to lie to the Holy Spirit and to keep back part of the proceeds of the land? While it remained unsold, did it not remain your own? And after it was sold, was it not at your disposal? How is it that you have contrived this deed in your heart? You have not lied to men but to God.' When Ananias heard these words, he fell down and died. A great fear came upon all who heard it. The young men arose and wrapped him up and carried him out and buried him.

"After an interval of about three hours his wife came in, not knowing what had happened. And Peter said to her, 'Tell me whether you sold the land for so much.' And she said, 'Yes, for so much.' But Peter said to her, 'How is it that you have agreed together to tempt the Spirit of the Lord? Hark, the feet of those that have buried your husband are at the door, and they will carry you out.' Immediately she fell down at his feet and died. When the young men came in they found her dead and they carried her out and buried her beside her husband. And great fear came upon the whole church, and upon all who heard of these things" (Acts 4:32-5:2).

It is not one's intention to dwell upon the judgment aspect of the story of Ananias and Sapphira. The days following Pentecost were days of revival, and in such times the Holy Spirit operates in unusual blessings towards the obedient and unusual severity towards the disobedient.* In the narrative are lessons for all to learn in all times.

It should first be noted that Ananias and Sapphira made a *voluntary* act of consecration. As the Apostle Peter said, while the land remained unsold, it was the owner's undisputed possession; and after it was sold, the money realized thereby was the owner's undisputed acquisition. No one told Ananias and Sapphira that they *must* sell their property in order to remain in Christian fellowship. No one *compelled* them to offer the proceeds to

---

* One saw a woman collapse under conviction in a revival meeting in Latvia. Even after she was carried out, no one knew her trouble, but the next day her sin was revealed.

the general fund of the infant Christian Church. Their maximum inducement was the power of godly example and exhortation. They saw others making a financial sacrifice, so they thought of a way whereby they might gain like approval without making the full sacrifice.

Likewise, the acts of consecration made by Christians today are all voluntary. No one is told that he must spend so much time in prayer in order to remain in fellowship. Neither is any one told that he must give a tenth or more in order to be recognized as a Christian. Nor is any one told that he must witness to so many people each week in order to prove that he is a believer. These things are done, but on account of godly example and exhortation rather than by compulsion.

Another noteworthy fact is that Ananias and Sapphira were unaware of the seriousness of their offence. They appeared to be unaware of any offence against God at all. The Apostle Peter told the husband, "You have not lied to men but to God!" One cannot imagine that Ananias and Sapphira sat together in conference and planned to tell a lie to the Holy Spirit. The Holy Spirit was far from their thoughts. The Apostle asked them how they had schemed such a thing in their hearts, but it does not seem likely that either husband or wife fancied themselves in a battle of wits against the Holy Spirit. They were unaware of His involvement.

So it is with Christians today. They scheme and plan and cheat and deceive in ways that involve the Holy Spirit, who cannot ignore broken vows. But the offenders are generally unaware of their offence. They think that it concerns themselves alone, and that failure is their own affair.

"How is it," asked the Apostle, "that you have agreed together to tempt the Spirit of the Lord?"

Ananias and Sapphira made an agreement together to sell their land and keep back part of the price, but it seems unlikely that they discussed the matter to the extent of saying, "Let us see how far we can provoke the Holy Spirit in this way!" The Holy Spirit was not in their thoughts.

And today many Christians, by keeping back part of the price of consecration, by making vows that are speedily broken, are guilty of provoking the Holy Spirit. No wonder they are making little or no progress in spiritual things. The fact that they have not suffered severely is but evidence of the long-suffering of God in times of spiritual decline.

In any case, Ananias and Sapphira suffered the extreme penalty as far as this life is concerned. There is dispute as to the future state of the erring church members. An ardent Philadelphian preacher has declared that Ananias and Sapphira were both genuine believers who offended the Holy Spirit and suffered a temporary judgment unaffecting their soul's eternal destiny. A zealous Chicagoan teacher affirms that, as Satan had filled the hearts of Ananias and Sapphira, they perished in judgment and went to perdition. There is neither time nor space to explore these lines of argument. There is agreement that the offenders suffered immediate breach of fellowship with God and His people, and that is what happens today to Christians who commit the same offence.

Fellowship, spiritual fellowship, is both vertical and horizontal. "If we say that we have fellowship with Him while we walk in darkness, we lie and do not live according to the truth." The vertical fellowship with God is broken by cheating in consecration, by broken vows. Everyone who has fellowship with God has fellowship with children of God. When the vertical connection is broken, the horizontal lines are snapped as well. Fellowship, spiritual fellowship, between Christians is broken as the result of broken vows. But fellowship is a word which is used in a sloppy way by Christians. They seem to think that ordinary social fellowship between believers is fellowship in the spiritual sense because both parties are professedly spiritual. This is not so. Spiritual fellowship is the presence of the Holy Spirit between believers. When one or both or all parties concerned have grieved the Holy Spirit, there is no real spiritual fellowship. It is noteworthy that a couple of Christians offending the Holy Spirit sustain their fellowship on a carnal level, generally by criticising maliciously the lives of other believers. They have no fellowship in love, but rather in common and carnal antipathies.

The penalty of trifling with the Holy Spirit is *breach of fellowship*. For a while, the friends of the offender may not notice that he no longer walks with God. For a while, the offender himself may be unaware of his breach of fellowship with God. The eyes accustom themselves to walking in the twilight of the sun that has set. But when judgment comes, the one who has trifled with God begins to realize that it is chilly after the sun has set, that he walks alone, and that he is stumbling in the murky darkness.

Had Ananias and Sapphira been better acquainted with their own Hebrew Scriptures, they would have found the warning of a very wise man against trifling with Deity. The Preacher in Ecclesiastes gives a plain warning against making vows which are not meant to be kept.*

"Watch your step when you go into the house of God; to draw near to listen is better

* The language of the Authorized King James Version is somewhat stilted: "Keep thy foot when thou goest to the house of God..."

than to offer the sacrifice of fools; for they do not realize that they are doing evil. Be not rash with your mouth, nor let your heart be hasty to utter a word before God, for God is in heaven, and you upon earth; therefore let your words be few... When you vow a vow to God, do not delay paying it; for He has no pleasure in fools. Pay what you vow. It is better that you should not vow than that you should vow and not pay. Let not your mouth lead you into sin, and do not say before the messenger that it was a mistake; why should God be angry at your voice, and destroy the work of your hands?" (Ecclesiastes 5:1-2, 4-6).

I endeavoured to enlist as an Air Force Chaplain in 1939. It was 1942 before my services were accepted. In due course, I received an extract of orders "by Direction of the President" ordering me to Active Duty. I went; I went promptly. True, I had volunteered; but once my services were accepted, I neither argued nor delayed nor disobeyed. I respected military authority.

Shortly after returning to the United Sates from Oxford, I made a slight error of judgment and parked my car in a doubtful place in Chicago's Loop. Upon my return, I found a ticket tied to the windshield wiper, informing me that I had transgressed an obscure parking regulation and was requested to appear at the Traffic Bureau on a day mentioned. I appeared. I neither argued nor delayed nor disobeyed. I respected the law.

The law has power to make me keep my obligations. How much more then should I respect the power of Almighty God? The trouble is that too many Christians presume upon the kindly fatherhood of God and forget that He is Lord of all.

Therefore "watch your steps when you go to God's house". The very thought of foolishness is sin to God, and it is foolish to trifle with vows.

"Be more ready to listen..." Too often prayer is a one-sided affair, degenerating into "Listen, Lord, Thy servant speaketh" instead of "Speak, Lord, Thy servant heareth!" It is better to listen to what God desires to tell us, for His calls are His enablings, than to open our big mouths and promise what vanity and pride prompt.

"Don't be rash...don't rush..." Weigh it first. When my wife returned from Oxford's Radcliffe with our second son David, I soon discovered that I was going to miss more sleep than in previous instances. My wife had a programme of feeding the infant—two o'clock, six o'clock, ten, two, six, ten, every four hours. My wife knew the programme, so did her doctor, so did the family, but apparently David didn't, nor did he seem to offer any alternative schedule.

So I found myself presented with two problems: one was how to get sufficient sleep, and the other was how to maintain my devotional schedule. A thought struck me one night. So I asked the Lord to let David sleep between his ten o'clock feeding and his six in the morning one, and I promised to get up at six in the morning for my quiet time. It was a wonderful idea. It seemed scarcely possible that it could happen. Alas, I did not tell my wife of my resolution, which showed my irresolution. I slept well, and the next waking moment was caused by the baby's whimper at three minutes before six. But...I went back to bed. Three mornings in succession this happened, but I found the warmth of bed too inviting compared to the chill of English morning, and the fire died in my heart. From then on the baby boy continued in his own affectionate but wholly unpredictable way, and I missed more sleep than ever.

It is better not to vow than to vow and not pay. Some vows originate in pride, and God resists the proud but gives grace to the humble. It is better to say "The Lord enabling me, I'll do thus and so" and then seek the necessary grace with a humble heart.

"Let not your mouth lead you into sin." If a man's tongue promises more than he fulfils, he thereby grieves the Holy Spirit. And the moment a man grieves the Spirit, he suffers a loss of sustaining grace, of which the Tempter is well aware. The wolf attacks the straggler, not the sheep that stays close by the shepherd. Broken vows bring spiritual weakness, and spiritual weakness brings temptation, and temptation sin.

Too often, when a Christian makes a vow and fails to keep it, he explains it away as a mistake, an error of judgment. In most cases, it is not a mistake, and the thing vowed is both worthy and possible. The error consists of falling short of the mark, which is definitely sin. There are occasions, however, when a Christian foolishly makes a promise which is incapable of fulfilment or unfortunate in its implications. The best thing to do is to confess the unwisdom of the matter to the Lord, seek His release, and ask for His guidance as to the proper course. But a vow should never be shrugged off.

"Why should God be angry at your voice, and destroy the work of your hands?" Not all prayer is acceptable. If one regards iniquity in one's heart, the Lord will not hear him. A broken vow is a sin of omission. It is also the commission of an affront to God. It must be confessed as sin before fellowship is completely restored. Otherwise, the discipline of God, the chastening of the Lord, begins to operate. It is necessary for the Lord to bring our schemes to nought in order that we may not waste time and effort in building of wood, hay and stubble. Our Friend becomes our opponent, not our enemy, and says "check" to each move until, checkmated, we begin again with Him.

What then are the vows that Christians customarily make to God in times of blessing and on special occasions? More time in prayer, more intercession for others, more devotional reading, more study, more personal witness, tithing of talents and money, better example to others, patience with children, personal purity, self-denial —these are the vows that are made in watchnight services, prayer meetings, evangelistic campaigns, deeper life conventions, missionary meetings, and the like. These vows go unfulfilled. Part of the price is kept back.

Until broken vows are mended, it is difficult to make progress along the way of consecration. Before seeking blessing from God, one should carefully consider in retrospect one's previous dealings with Deity. It is not enough that no offence was meant. It is not enough that no deceit was planned in advance. The sin against God arises from the most serious transgression of any commandment, that of nursing a coldness of heart towards God Himself.

CHAPTER TWO

FORGIVENESS OF SINS

MANY years ago, I heard of the capture of a young burglar, caught red-handed by the police. The burglar was a young married man, with two children, so his younger brother went to the police and offered to take the offender's place. The police sergeant refused point-blank to let him substitute for his brother.

"You did not commit the crime," he said, "and we cannot allow you to suffer the punishment. It wouldn't be right."

That incident illustrates a difficulty which plagued my young mind for many years. I had been converted through my mother's witness given me on my ninth birthday. She had told me that Christ died for my sins, that He was wounded for my transgressions. I believed it in my heart. What's more, it worked out in my life, and with conversion I received an assurance that my sins were truly blotted out. But I could not understand it in my mind. That the innocent often suffered for the guilty, I knew it to be so; but I could not understand at first how God in justice could plan it so. Light came many years later.

I heard Bishop Stephen Neill tell a hushed house of Oxford students that he had not fully understood the meaning of the Cross until he heard an Indian Christian evangelist tell the story of the Prodigal Son in a market place in South India. The evangelist pointed out that when the prodigal revolted against the husks of the swine, he was sorry for himself but scarcely understood the cost of forgiveness. Even as he walked his weary way home, reciting to himself the apology "I have sinned against heaven and in thy sight", he could not have understood the enormity of his offence. Even when his father rushed out to meet him, even during the welcome-home banquet, he did not fully understand. It was not until some days afterwards that the prodigal noticed that his father's hair had turned white in his absence. Then he appreciated the cost of forgiveness.

My mind went back to the days when I used to play ball "out the back" behind our house in the Ormeau suburb of Belfast. I was seven years old. Diagonally across the back from our house was the house of an unfortunate man, unfortunate only in the sense that his windows were always being broken by stray balls. He should have moved his house, we thought. One day he came charging out of the house, waving an indignant fist: "The next one of you kids breaks my window—I'll break your ear!"

We fled in distress. There was not much good in arguing with him. He had a one-track mind and would not listen to reason. And who was the next one to break his windows? I did not even stop to pick up the bat. The ball was doubtless under one of his beds, beyond recall. I ran instinctively for the shelter of home, but the news of my misdemeanour preceded me. My father was in the kitchen and grabbed my wrist before I could make a quiet exit. He insisted that I accompany him to the scene of my offence.

"I've brought you the culprit that broke your window," he told the man.

The man glared at me. Then he turned to my father in a more reasonable tone of voice.

"Look here, Mr. Orr, I know that kids can't help breaking windows. I used to break them when I was a kid myself. But it isn't right that any time a window gets broken round this back it has to be my window. I'm willing to forgive the kids, but somebody's got to pay for it!"

So my father paid the man, who told me I was forgiven but not to do it again. And I carried away a lasting impression in my mind concerning forgiveness—somebody must pay for it. That is the first principle of forgiveness—someone must pay for it.

Twenty years later, an Irish friend of mine borrowed a sum of money from me. He had been gambling and was in danger of losing his job. He agreed to pay me back in weekly instalments, but never did. I felt annoyed with the fellow for a couple of years. Finally I decided to forgive him. But who suffered? The debtor or the creditor? The sinner or the sinned against? Obviously the sinned against. I could have taken him to court, in which case he would have suffered. How much would he have suffered? The amount that he owed me! Instead I forgave him, and so I suffered; and I suffered the amount that he owed me, that I had forgiven him. Thus I learned a second principle of forgiveness— the one who forgives is the one who suffers.

Such reflections made the Cross more real to me. It was necessary for someone to suffer, for someone had to pay. But the one who forgives is the one who suffers, so it was necessary for Christ to suffer. Moses could hot have suffered the Cross, nor Jeremiah, nor Peter, nor Paul. It had to be God, the only One who could forgive. And Christ Jesus was God made manifest in the flesh.

No theory of the atonement is complete in itself. Certainly the moral influence theory is true, but incomplete.

We sing:

> *Were the whole realm of nature mine,*
>   *That were an offering far too small:*
> *Love so amazing, so divine,*
>   *Demands my life, my soul, my all.*

Yet moral influence is not the whole truth. Even the substitutionary theory of the Cross is incomplete. The fact of the Cross is greater than any particular theory of it, or all such theories together.

It is possible to sum up the teaching of the forgiveness of sins of the unregenerate man thus:

Basis	The Cross
Price	Nothing
Conditions	Conversion
Method	Faith
Forfeiture	Judgment

The Cross is the Basis of God's forgiveness of sins. The Price of the sinner is nothing. God attaches a Condition: "Repent and be converted that your sins might be blotted out." The Method of appropriation by the sinner is by faith. And the sinner who forfeits the forgiveness of God faces his sins at the Great Judgment.

But what about the forgiveness of the sins of the believer? There is much misunderstanding in this. A university student, member of an evangelical church, once protested to me: "Why should I confess the untruth I told last week? I was converted years ago, and I am still a believer, so all my sins, past, present and future, are already forgiven."

The young lady missed the distinction between the forgiveness of sins against salvation and the forgiveness of sins against fellowship. This is a common misapprehension. Some good people refuse to use the Lord's Pattern Prayer because of the phrase: "Forgive us our trespasses as we forgive those who trespass against us." They say that the sins of a sinner are forgiven not on that basis but freely, therefore the prayer is not for today. They forget that our Lord was talking to His own disciples, and that the prayer concerns fellowship and not salvation. God forgives our sins against fellowship upon different conditions than conversion; otherwise we would need to become converted again and again, as often as we fell short of God's mark.

One of the most spiritual women it has been my privilege to meet had suffered severely at the hands of the Nazis. When she was finally released, she left the concentration camp with bitterness in her heart against the whole race of Germans. She found it difficult to forgive. Being devoted to God, she contemplated missionary service, and was willing to go anywhere, from Shanghai to the Sahara, but not to Germany. The petition in the Lord's Prayer frightened her: "Forgive us our trespasses as we forgive those who trespass against us!" She began to feel that if she could not forgive the Germans, God would not forgive her.

Knowing that she had been brought up in a strong Calvinistic atmosphere, I asked her: "If you continued to hold bitterness in your heart towards the Germans, would your soul's salvation be in jeopardy?"

Her theology told her "no!" but her heart was confused. I quietly showed her that the forgiveness of sins referred to in our Lord's Prayer concerned the failures of His children who were already born again, that they were sins against fellowship rather than sins against salvation.

This distinction must always be kept in mind. The message for the believer concerning the forgiveness of sins against fellowship is surely found in the words of 1 John 1:5-9:

> "This is the message which we have heard from Him and proclaim to you, that God is light and in Him is no darkness at all. If we say we have fellowship with Him while we walk in darkness, we lie and do not live according to the truth; but if we walk in the light, as He is in the light, we have fellowship with one another, and the blood of Jesus His Son cleanses us from all sin. If we say we have no sin, we deceive ourselves, and the truth is not in us. If we confess our sins, He is faithful and just, and will forgive us our sins and cleanse us from all unrighteousness."

From this passage, it is seen that the forgiveness of sins against fellowship is based upon the Cross, the Blood of Jesus Christ, which not only cleanses us from sin in purchasing our salvation, but continues to cleanse us. The Greek present continuous tense is used herein. Therefore the Basis of forgiveness is again the Cross. To the erring believer the Price is nothing, for God will heal our backsliding and forgive us freely. The Condition is, not conversion, but confession. The Method of appropriation of forgiveness by the believer is by faith. And the result of forfeiting forgiveness is again judgment, but this time either self-judgment (immediately or following Divine chastisement) or the Judgment Seat of Christ, where an account will be rendered by all believers of the deeds done in the body.

A summary and comparison may be made thus:

THE FORGIVENESS OF SINS

Unbeliever	Subject	Believer
Salvation	Object	Fellowship
The Cross	Basis	The Cross
Nothing	Price	Nothing
Conversion	Conditions	Confession
Faith	Method	Faith
Judgment	Forfeiture	Judgment

In comparing the forgiveness of sins of the unbeliever in relation to salvation with the forgiveness of sins of the believer in relation to fellowship, it will be seen that the Basis is the same Cross of Christ, with punctiliar application in the first instance and linear in the second. The Price is the same to the unbeliever and believer: it is not by works, although works may follow. The method of appropriation in both cases is the same, for we accept forgiveness by faith. The Forfeit is the same, judgment, although in the first instance it refers to the Great White Throne, where eternal life is forfeited, and in the second instance to the Judgment Seat of Christ, where rewards are forfeited.

The crux of the matter for the Christian is obviously the question of confession of sins. "If we confess our sins, He is faithful and just to forgive us our sins and cleanse us from all unrighteousness... and the blood of Jesus His Son cleanses us from all sin." Put negatively, if we do not confess our sins (against fellowship), God will not forgive us our sins nor cleanse us from unrighteousness.

Confession of sins is a neglected doctrine and only comes into its rightful place in times of revival, when the Holy Spirit comes in doubly convicting power, and makes it impossible for the erring believer to have any peace until he confesses his wrong where necessary.

CHAPTER THREE

CONFESSION OF SINS

C LEAR teaching concerning the confessing of sins by Christians is one of the most neglected doctrines of today. Such confession is taught in Scripture and manifest in every great spiritual awakening. Why then is there such ignorance, prejudice, and misunderstanding and neglect?

There appears to be two main objections in the minds of those who are critical of confession of sins; first, a protest against the public confession of sins better dealt with in private; and second, a denial that either public or private confession of sins is ever necessary.

In the first instance, the objection may be met by clear and simple scriptural teaching regarding the limits of confession. As for the second, the necessity of confession of sins to parties concerned is so clear that the very vehemence of objection must be attributed to unwillingness of the subject to put right serious matters requiring adjustment. In my own experience of real revival over a period of fifteen years and in many countries, I heard no actual transgression of the limits of decency or good taste where the scriptural teaching was propounded or the leading of the Spirit clearly followed; and it has been a sad discovery that many pastors and teachers and evangelists who hotly opposed confession of sins had their opposition explained too often by private complaint or public scandal.

Before seeking the relevant texts in Scripture, it seems good to state a maxim of confession to set at rest the minds of those who are uneasy about it. *Let the circle of the offence committed be the circle of the confession made!* In other words, secret sins should always be secretly confessed, private sins should be privately confessed, and open sins should be openly confessed. Sins between the individual soul and God are defined as secret as distinct from private sins involving other individuals.

(1) Specific Confession
Charles Grandison Finney, the most scholarly of the great American evangelists, has written:

> "A revival of religion may be expected when Christians begin to confess their sins to one another. At other times they confess in a general manner, as if they are only half in earnest. They may do it in eloquent language, but it does not mean anything. But when there is an ingenuous breaking down, and a pouring out of the heart in confession of sin, the floodgates will soon burst open, and salvation will flow over the place."

The same emphasis is found in the writings of the renowned Canadian Presbyterian missionary, Jonathan Goforth, leader of great movements in Korea and Manchuria. It can be found in the records of great awakenings in every generation and country that has experienced the moving of the Spirit. Confession of sins must be specific and not general.

This principle of specific confession is clearly taught (Leviticus 5:5):

> "And it shall be, when he shall be guilty in one of these things, that he shall confess that he has sinned in that thing."

It costs nothing for a church member to admit in a prayer meeting: "I am not what I ought to be." It costs no more to say: "I ought to be a better Christian." It costs something to say: "I have been a trouble-maker in this church." It costs something to say: "I have bitterness of heart towards certain leaders, to whom I shall definitely apologise."

While it is true that human hearts possess attitudes towards sin which can be described as *general*, all acts of sin are *particular* and should be confessed in a particular way. A sinner might be overwhelmed by so many specific convictions of sin that he does not know where to begin. He should begin with his besetting sin, about which he will feel most conviction. The exhortation to confess our sins is clearly progressive: "If we keep on confessing our sins."

(2) Responsible Confession

Achan, a soldier in Joshua's army, disobeyed military orders and divine commands by looting silver and gold and clothing, so, with divine blessing withdrawn, the armies of Israel tasted humiliating defeat at the hands of a small enemy garrison. By lots Joshua located the looter, and told him (Joshua 7:19):

> "My son, give, I pray thee, glory to the Lord God of Israel, and make confession unto Him; and tell me what thou hast done; hide it not from me."

Confession was first due to God against whom the sin had been committed, but it next became due to persons affected by the sin, for the blessing of God had been withheld on account of one sinner. Achan made responsible confession.

Shortly before the Bethel College Awakening in Minnesota in April 1949, with which began the mid-century series of college revivals in the United States, I was engaged in evangelism under the auspices of an evangelical student group at a university in the Middle West. I was greatly heartened by the noonday prayer meetings of the students on behalf of their unconverted fellows, but greatly dismayed that not one so prayed for made decision, although other contacts did. The president of the group did not attend many meetings because of preoccupation, his wife being in a nursing home with their firstborn. Then someone told me privately that these otherwise admirable Christians had been married only five months. This unfortunate happening bothered me less in spirit than the fact that six months before this student had accepted election to the presidency, which was hypocrisy. Public confession of pre-marital relationship seemed unnecessary, but he should have confessed openly his hypocrisy and unworthiness to the group and offered his resignation. And there were those who were prepared to re-nominate him once the faults were confessed. He never did confess his fault, and the Lord's judgment became unavoidable.

(3) Thorough Confession

In Proverbs 28:13 is a clear statement on confession:

> "He that covereth his sins shall not prosper, but whoso confesseth and forsaketh them shall have mercy."

Once the conviction of sin has been quenched, there is a tendency for the sinner to cover or bury anything that remains of unpleasant memory. The work of the Holy Spirit in pre-revival judgment is to reveal such things.

I recall crossing the Soviet Russian frontier west of Leningrad. The Customs officer quickly inspected my baggage and passed me, but the lady who followed me, a Russian American, appeared to be trying to smuggle in all sorts of things for her relatives there, and the Customs officer began a thorough search of all her baggage, bringing to light all sorts of things that had been *hidden* or *forgotten* or *both*. So it is with conviction.

The Proverbs link confessing and forsaking. Some confessions are not thorough. They are too general. They are not made to the persons concerned. They neglect completely the necessary restitution. Or they make no provision for a different course of conduct in which the sin is forsaken. They are endeavours for psychological relief.

It is not enough to announce in school that one has cheated. Academic restitution ought to be offered the teacher concerned. It is not enough to admit that one has been a thief. The stolen goods should be taken back. It is not enough to confess that one has been malicious. The malicious falsehoods or slanders ought to be confessed to the person wronged.

I have regretful memories of Christian Endeavour Consecration meetings in which I and most others glibly confessed that we were failures and that Christ was not a failure. So long as I was not specific, and made no real attempt to break the power of besetting sin, I got nowhere.

(4) Private Confession

Concerning private confession, confession made by individual to individual as distinct from secret or public confession, the clearest statement is found in the words of our Lord, in Matthew 5:23-24:

"So if you are offering your gift at the altar, and there remember that your brother has something against you, leave your gift there before the altar and go; first be reconciled to your brother, and then come and offer your gift."

Most Christians display a preference for confession in secret before God, even concerning matters which involve other people. To confess to God seems to them to be the easiest way out. If offenders were really conscious of the presence of God, even secret confession of private sin would have a salutary effect. Alas, most offenders merely commune with themselves instead of making contact with God, who refuses their prayers under certain conditions.

In the words of our Lord, it is clear that sin involving another person should be confessed to that person. The offering referred to in Hebrew sacrifice was an offering accompanied by direct confession of sin to God for wilful or inadvertent transgression. Thus it is underlined that it is not enough to confess the sin to God alone, but to any person hurt thereby. And persons can be hurt in various ways.

Sins against sexual purity are more involved. In fornication, here defined as unchastity between unmarried man and woman, the convicted person should renounce the sin to his partner and make sure that the temptation is never repeated. In adultery, here defined as unchastity between married persons not married to each other, the convicted person should urge the other to put the matter right with the other's wronged spouse. The utmost discretion is needed in marital adjustment. It would certainly be unfair for a seducer to enjoy the pleasures of seduction and then glibly urge his victim to put things right with her husband. He should offer to take the blame and make things easier for his victim. In any case, an unfaithful husband or wife should consider the *timing* and circumstances of confession, and should avoid unnecessary damage to the marriage, if the marriage can be redeemed by forgiveness which should be sought earnestly and humbly.

A sinner may offend someone who is not a party to the act by consent. To use offensive language to a second person in the presence of a third requires an apology to both second and third parties. The same thing applies in apologising for loss of temper to all witnesses, or for bad example.

One might think that the initiative in reconciliation belongs to the sinner rather than the offended. Certainly the responsibility for confession is the sinner's, but in matters involving two Christians, the initiative in reconciliation belongs to the more spiritual, the offended:

> "If your brother sins against you, go and tell him his fault, between you and him alone. If he listens to you, you have gained your brother. But if he does not listen, take one or two others along with you, that every word may be confirmed by the evidence of two or three witnesses. If he refuses to listen to them, tell it to the church; and if he refuses to listen even to the church, let him be to you as a heathen..." (Matthew 18:15-17)

(5) Open Confession

There is definite exhortation of open confession in Scripture, and although no limits are mentioned, unwise open confession seems to be as implicitly prohibited as would be insincere, vicious, or profane confession. Common sense tells us that descriptive details of a scheme of cheating without detection or of impure acts would prove a temptation to others and should never be mentioned.

The well-known pastor of a renowned New England church told me that an officer of his church, under suggestion from a popular movement, asked permission to make a statement to the congregation. It was humble and sincere, but it concerned sexual sin so distasteful that even the most spiritual hearers could never dissociate the memory of it from him in later days, even though they rejoiced in his deliverance from it.

Almost all sexual offences are either secret or private and should be confessed in secret or in private. If the burden is too much to bear, a confession can be shared with a pastor, doctor, or wise friend of the same sex. The Scripture discourages even the naming of immorality among believers, and says that it is a shame even to speak of things done in secret thereby.

Open confession was practised during the baptizing of John in the Jordan, and following the preaching of Paul in Ephesus. It had limits, no doubt. The manifest need for limiting open confession should not become an excuse for prohibiting open confession, for the commandment is clear in James 5:16:

"Therefore confess your sins to one another, and pray for one another, that you may be healed. The prayer of a righteous man has great power in its effects."

The peerless Greek scholar, Dr. A. T. Robertson, has written that confession to God already is assumed in this exhortation, and that public confession of certain sins to one another in the meetings is greatly helpful in many ways. Christians utterly unacquainted with the Greek should note that, although the King James Authorized Version uses the word "faults", the more ancient manuscripts and more modern translations use "sins". The sense of the Greek verb "confess" implies group confession, not private confession between one individual and another, literally "ones to others".

Group confession brings psychological relief, but the motive should not be that. We make confession to obtain prayer to gain spiritual healing, and the Greek word for healing given here is used elsewhere for the healing of the soul as well as of physical sickness. Such group confession is not hurtful, for the individual is encouraged thereby to forsake the sin and is helped by the knowledge that sympathetic friends will pray for him, while others in the group are challenged to bring their own problems to the light. In recent days, there have been widely read reports of a few unwise public confessions among an overwhelming number of restrained ones. The leaders have told me that their conviction was that these few confessions were unwise, and only fear of intruding into a work of grace held back their advice or rebuke. It should have been given beforehand.

(6) Cleansing Confession
From the word of 1 John 1:9:

"If we confess our sins, He is faithful and just, and will forgive us our sins and cleanse us from all unrighteousness..."

It seems that the forgiveness and cleansing of sins hindering our fellowship with God depend upon our confession of the same. The price of blessing involves the heart-searching of the Spirit, candid admission of failure, immediate confession to God, and subsequent confession to persons involved. The circle of sin committed should be the circle of the confession made. The spirit who searches the heart will guide the confession.

CHAPTER FOUR

THE SEARCHING OF HEART

THE Holy Spirit is the author of revival, both individual and collective. It is His ministry that brings a believer to a sense of need; that brings a church to repentance; that brings a whole community to hunger of heart. And yet the Holy Spirit is, comparatively speaking, the unknown quantity and personality in the Godhead.

According to Christ Himself, the ministry of the Holy Spirit is to convince the world of sin, unrighteousness, and judgment. Many believers mistakenly rely upon their consciences alone rather than upon conscience enlightened by the Word of God and quickened by the Spirit of God.

The work of the Holy Spirit, therefore, is to show the sinner how far he has fallen short; to show him also the standard of righteousness in Christ; and to warn him of inevitable judgment. It is noteworthy that the Holy Spirit performs a parallel work in the life of a Christian, convicting him of carnality, which is falling short; spurring him to practical sanctification, which is appropriating the righteousness of Christ for everyday living; and warning him of the judgment seat of Christ, where he may lose his rewards.

It is to the Holy Spirit that the Christian must look if he is ever to find a place of revival for his own soul. Spiritual blessing for the believer is dependent upon the confession of sins and the restitution of wrongs. But confession, in turn, is dependent upon conviction, and conviction comes with the searching of the heart by the Holy Spirit.

The most effective prayer for a heart-hungry believer is an Old Testament petition found in the Psalms of David (Psalm 139:23-24):

> *Search me, O God, and know my heart;*
> *Try me, and know my thoughts;*
> *And see if there be a way of grief in me,*
> *And lead me in the way of eternity.*

I never fully understood the significance of this prayer until I heard the verse translated into the Scandinavian tongues. There the word "search" is rendered "ransack". It takes little imagination to picture the thoroughness of a job of ransacking as compared to mere searching. Ransacking turns things upside down and brings to light things that are hidden or forgotten. In times of backsliding, the Spirit is quenched, and as life goes on the natural tendency is for a convicted person to forget the unpleasant episode. In conviction of sin, the debris of ordinary living is swept aside and the offending thing is brought to attention. Hence, if believers are to avoid superficiality in confession, a thorough ransacking of the heart is necessary.

The petition is definite: "Search *me*!" Too often the more spiritual members of a church or group are more aware of the glaring faults of their less spiritual neighbours than they are of their own shortcomings. The proper emphasis is found in the negro spiritual song:

> *"Not my brother, nor my sister,*
> *But it's me, O Lord,*
> *Standing in the need of prayer..."*

The disciples did not say: "Is it Peter...or James... or Judas?" but: "Lord, is it I?" There is a time for every purpose under the heaven, and there is a time for healthy introspection. Our prayers go unheard until we cease regarding iniquity in our hearts, and only by probing the heart is the sin dragged out to the healing light.

It is significant that the petition is addressed to Deity. Neither pastor nor psychiatrist, physician nor psychologist, friend nor enemy, stranger nor familiar self can adequately search the heart for sin. Sin is an offence against God, and only God can reveal its offensiveness.

To a consultant, most inquirers reveal what suits their feelings. Be he ever so clever, a well-trained pastor or psychiatrist is limited by his own prejudices or training. The information brought for analysis is limited by the seeker's feelings, and the human judgment brought to the case is limited by the adviser's ideas. Man makes inadequate analysis and diagnosis. God makes no mistakes.

Self is an even poorer judge of sin than a consultant. Man is utterly incapable of searching his own heart. Man rationalizes his sin. I remember well an acquaintance in Illinois who appeared to be a pathological liar. He told lies so often and so repeatedly that he came to believe them himself. No one can be trusted to examine his own heart.

It is the heart and the thoughts that need searching. Some people commit sin in the warmth of affections, desires or passions. Others are cold-blooded about contemplating transgression. God searches the heart and tries the thoughts. As a man thinks in his heart, so is he. Murder begins in hatred, stealing in covetousness, adultery in impurity of thought.

And lest anyone excuse himself because he is not conscious of gross sin, be it noted that the prayer adds the entreaty: "See if there is a *way of grief* in me!" Anything which grieves the Holy Spirit of God is a hindrance to blessing, and stands in the way of revival.

And what is *the way everlasting*? Primarily, it is the Way, Christ. If we say we walk in darkness, we lie and do not act according to the truth. Walking in the way everlasting means walking in the light, it means walking in the truth. And Christ is the Way, the Truth and the Life.

The Searching of the Holy Spirit shows believers how they have strayed from the way, and confession of sin leads them back to the path of fellowship. This in itself is spiritual revival.

Is the Searching of the Heart by the Spirit utterly independent of the co-operation of the seeking Christian? By no means. A believer may fully co-operate with the Spirit in the heart-searching. First, he must recognise his needy state and humbly acknowledge that his condition is not God's will. Then he must pray and specifically ask the Spirit to search his heart. Not only must he continue in prayer, in which the Spirit may convict him, but he must also give diligent attention to the reading of the Word, especially such passages which apply to his need or condition, for thereby also the Spirit convicts. Just as much, he must hand over the keys to the vaults of memory, and try to recall the acts or tendencies which derailed his spiritual life. He may also seek the counsel of a friend, for sometimes the Spirit puts His rebuke in the mouth of a friend. He may even examine the unkind and unpleasant things said about him by his critics and enemies, who may be telling the truth, even though saying it maliciously. Of one thing the believer may be certain; the Holy Spirit never leaves a seeking heart untouched. He is ever willing for surgery and healing.

CHAPTER FIVE

SINS OF THE TONGUE

JAMES, the Lord's brother, devotes a chapter of his practical Epistle to the subject of Control of the Tongue. The chapter can be read without deep conviction unless the Christian is willing to let the Holy Spirit search his heart for manifestations of the sins of the tongue, using the injunctions of Scripture as well as personal prayer.

Anger

While anger, or bad temper, is a sin of the spirit in its primary sense, it so often results in the loss of control of the tongue that it is here considered as a sin of the tongue. Anger has many varieties: indignation, irritation, impatience, vexation, bitterness, exasperation, resentment, passion, choler, temper, wrath, ire, rage, fury—and these may express themselves in all sorts of ill-tempered words, ranging from the cold acid of sarcasm to the hot flame of fury. Every expression of anger is full of danger, not excepting even the most noble form of indignation.

It is very easy to remember that, if one is in the right, one need not lose one's temper; and if one is in the wrong, one can't afford to do it. Angry words never improve any situation.

The Psalmist advised his friends (37:8) to cease from anger and to forsake wrath. The world's wisest man declared that one slow to wrath demonstrates great understanding, but a quick-tempered man displays his own foolishness (Proverbs 14:29).

Everyone knows that a soft answer turns away wrath, but grievous words stir up anger (15:1). A discrete man puts off his anger, but an angry one gets nothing but punishment (19:11, 19). An angry woman is harder to put up with than life in the wilderness; and an angry man is so dangerous that one should have neither friendship nor company with him (21:19, 22:24). Wrath is cruel and anger outrageous (27:4). So goes the warning of the writer of Proverbs; so also Ecclesiastes (7:9).

Our Lord in His Sermon on the Mount declared that anyone becoming angry with his brother is liable to judgment. The New Testament continues the emphasis of the Old on the subject of anger. The advice of the Apostle Paul, "be angry but do not sin", is not a command to be angry, but a prohibition against sinning in anger (Ephesians 4:26). In other words, the Apostle warned the Christians: "If you let yourself get angry, be careful that you do not sin!" In the same letter, the Apostle told his friends in the Ephesian Church (4:31) to put away all bitterness, wrath, anger, and clamour, and he repeats the advice to the Colossians (3:8).

Christians excuse their bad temper in different ways. Some among the more carnal are actually somewhat proud of their uncontrolled spirit. I have heard a famous speaker describe from the pulpit how he lost his temper, and his account of the incidents showed not a trace of repentance, rather an ignorant pride. The more spiritual Christians, knowing that ill-temper is an offence, find a euphemism for their own faults in describing them. One of the most common is to attribute bad temper to the nerves, making an infirmity out of fault.

It is far better to admit the fault, to repent and confess, to forsake it and to make humble apology for it. God can give victory along the lines of greatest defeat. Bad temper controlled becomes good temper, not absence of temper. A person with a controlled temper can achieve much more than one without reserves of spirit.

Profanity

The third commandment states:

> "Thou shalt not take the name of the Lord thy God in vain; for the Lord will not hold him guiltless that taketh His name in vain" (Exodus 20:7).

The commandment of Christ tells us:

> "Do not swear at all, either by heaven; for it is the throne of God, or by the earth, for it is His footstool, or by Jerusalem, for it is the city of the great king. And do not swear by your head, for you cannot make one hair white or black. Let what you say be simply "yes" or "no"; anything more than this comes from evil" (Matthew 5:34-37).

As a chaplain in the Forces overseas, I can say quite simply that to me profanity was a sorer trial than any terror of war. Profanity included vulgarity, lewdness, sacrilege, blasphemy, and horrible mixtures of all four. By far the worst was the taking in vain of the name of the Lord. The men used to tell me that they meant nothing by it, that they were not even thinking of God when they thus mentioned His name. Nevertheless, the Lord did not hold them guiltless while taking His name in vain.

I found that men swore either to shock people, to be mean, or to hide inferiority. Their profanity showed a lack of education, breeding and character. It lowered self-respect, cheapened the better things and defiled the whole personality. It shocked people of good taste, provoked contempt, fouled the atmosphere, set a bad example, and disqualified men for decent society. Worst of all, it offended God.

Upon return to civilian life, I discovered that many men who no longer moved in circles where foul language prevailed switched to minced oaths. Unfortunately, a large number of professing Christians adopted the same silly and subtle vocabulary of simulated swear-words. According to the Webster Unabridged Dictionary, such words as "gosh" or "gee" are minced oaths, euphemisms for "God" or "Jesus". A minced oath is recognizable by similarity of consonants or vowels occurring in the original oath. Everyone should recognize "darn" as a substitute for "damn", "heck" as a substitute for "hell", and other words as a substitute for expressions too crude to be hinted at in print. Expletives beginning with "g", "j", or "c" should always be suspect. Expressions beginning with the preposition "by" are nearly always substitute swear words even if their point is blunted by the use of some derelict god or other ridiculous name.

For a Christian to excuse his substitute oaths by saying that he means nothing by them, and is not even thinking of the significance of the words, sounds like the excuse of profane swearers overseas. It jars one's tender memory to hear professing Christians, including leaders, use words which had an ugly origin in vulgarity or lewdness. One even hears nice old ladies use expressions which in their original form would shock the users speechless. The best way to avoid using language which sounds profane to the initiate is to avoid using extravagant expletives. The obedient Christian wants to avoid the very semblance of evil. Experience has proved that a new convert can eliminate minced oaths.

Let the person who is inclined to scoff at condemnation of fashionable expletives remember that Christ Himself taught that unnecessarily garnished language is a product of evil. The Lord's brother, James, taught that the man who controls his tongue can control his whole personality, so let the scoffer try to eliminate his questionable epithets for a month. If he cannot do it, he is in bondage to a bad habit: if he can do it, he will find that the habit is unnecessary. The English language has the richest vocabulary in the world, yet some verbal cripples have to hobble along with questionable crutch words.

> "Let no evil talk come out of your mouths, but only such as is good for edifying, as fits the occasion, that it may impart grace to those who hear; and do not grieve the Holy Spirit..." (Ephesians 4:29-30)

Lying

I doubt if anything is more clearly condemned in Scripture than lying. Christ characterizes the Devil as a liar thus (John 8:44):

> "When he lies, he speaks according to his own nature, for he is a liar and the father of lies."

The Genesis story attributes the fall of man to the lying and deceit of the Serpent, and the Revelation predicts that all liars shall have their lot in the lake of fire, the second death.

The Ten Commandments condemn false witness, and the Lord told Moses and the Children of Israel directly "neither lie to one another" (Leviticus 19:2). The Apostle Paul echoes the same word: "Do not lie one to another" (Colossians 3:9); and: "Therefore, putting away falsehood, let every one speak the truth with his neighbour" (Ephesians 4:25).

The Psalms condemn lying, and so do the Proverbs. The Prophets warn against it, and so do the Apostles. The references to lying in the Bible are too numerous for comment. Obviously lying is a serious sin.

Among worldly people, lying is not so regarded. People tell each other without a blush of lies that they have told for their own advantage, and, providing no other point of honour is outraged, the hearer is not offended by the bragging.

On the other hand, only the most carnal of Christians will unblushingly admit lying. Conscience is outraged by downright lying. Most Christians will make an effort not to tell a lie, but if circumstances prove embarrassing, many will not hesitate to lie their way out of difficulty and consider it the lesser of two evils, the other evil in their opinion being the consequences of admitting the truth.

Stricter Christians, however, will avoid lying; and despise and distrust those who practise it. Some of the more spiritual Christians find their temptation in equivocation, exaggeration, under-statement and similar giving of wrong impressions. All these shortcomings of the truth are lying. Charles Grandison Finney, who applied a fine mind and legal training to his evangelism, wrote his opinion pungently:

> "Understand now what lying is. Any species of designed deception. If the deception be not designed, it is not lying. But if you design to make an impression contrary to the naked truth, you lie. Put down all those cases you can recollect. Do not call them by any soft name. God calls

them Lies, and charges you with Lying, and you had better charge yourself correctly.

"How innumerable are the falsehoods perpetrated every day in business, and in social intercourse, by words, and looks, and actions designed to make an impression on others, for selfish reasons that is contrary to the truth."

Lying, to my mind, is any calculated form of deceit. It is possible to tell what the truth is and yet convey a lying impression. For example, an American evangelist came to visit me at Oxford University, which was many thousands of miles away from his home. Anyone in Oxford could have seen him running around the place with a blonde. Were I not to add immediately that his wife was the blonde concerned I would be guilty of lying. Suppression of pertinent parts of the truth can become lying. Telling what is not true does not necessarily constitute lying. At the moment of writing, I would be ready to inform any inquirer that my brother is in London. A long-distance telephone call might prove me wrong for the moment, but as long as I said what I believed was true I would be innocent of lying. In certain circumstances, however, to discover that one had made a statement that was not true requires correction of the wrong impression.

Lying lips are an abomination to the Lord. The worst form appears to be lying with regard to spiritual matters. It was Satan who filled the heart of Ananias to lie to the Holy Spirit. The fact that Ananias did not realize it was lying to God did not excuse him.

Criticism

The word criticism is defined as either "the act

of criticizing, especially unfavourably" or "the art of judging with knowledge and propriety". The latter is a virtue and the former is a vice with which it is proposed to deal, for it is none other than the apostolically condemned sin of *malice*, for which Christians use the softer word *criticism*.

There is a great difference between constructive criticism and destructive criticism. A loving wife will criticize her husband without any unloving thought arising. A loving parent will criticize his child without any cessation of affection. A loving brother will criticize in the same way, always with the purpose of help and not hurt. But the root of unkind criticism is selfishness, a selfishness which thrives upon depreciating others, therefore wholly negative.

Years ago, in New Zealand, I received a letter from a Christian leader in Canada, apologising for having criticized me so unkindly that he had actually persuaded people not to go and hear me preach in the Massey Hall in Toronto. There were four pages of sincere apology, and only the last few lines gave any clue concerning the nature of the criticism made. In those days, being only twenty-three years of age, I had grown a moustache to hide my immaturity. The Toronto brother felt that a fellow sporting a moustache like that could not be living very close to the Lord! Although I wrote a letter of forgiveness immediately, I chuckled for days over the petty nature of the criticism. Then it suddenly dawned upon my mind that the real reason for his critical attitude was not the moustache, however much it outraged his sense of propriety: it was lack of love for a brother in Christian service. I never forgot the lesson.

Surely lack of love for the brethren is the root of all the unhappy criticism and divisions in the

Christian fellowship. We do not practise or permit criticism of those who are dear to us, including ourselves. We criticise those who mean less to us, and in so doing demonstrate our shortcomings in Christian love.

In the matter of criticism which is intended to be constructive, the critic should ask himself several questions before passing on a criticism to the one criticised. First: "Am I willing for an equally severe examination of my own behaviour?" Second: Is my motive in making criticism sincere love for the person concerned and concern for the Lord's name? Third: "Is the criticism calculated to correct the fault or merely relieve my irritation? A criticism failing to pass these tests is more likely to harm than help.

Likewise, when a Christian feels it is his duty or is asked to give his opinion of the behaviour of another Christian, he should test his motives, not only with the first and second questions foregoing, but another: "Would I be willing to make the criticism to the person criticised?" Or: "Have I tried to correct the fault of my brother?"

The words of our Lord are clear:

"Judge not, that ye be not judged. For with the judgment you pronounce you will be judged, and the measure you give will be the measure you get. Why do you see the speck that is in your brother's eye, but do not notice the log that is in your own eye? Or how can you say to your brother, 'Let me take the speck out of your eye,' when there is the log in your own eye? You hypocrite, first take the log out of your own eye, and then you will see clearly to take the speck out of your brother's eye" (Matthew 7:1-5).

This advice does not mean that we should be

tolerant of evil, but rather that we should always deal with the wrongdoing in our lives first. The Apostle Paul warned the Corinthian Christians not to associate with anyone calling himself a Christian but disgracing the name. He added (I Corinthians 5:12):

> "Is it not those inside the church whom you are to judge?"

The same Apostle (Ephesians 4:31) urges believers not only to put away all malice, but he specifies *slander*. In law, the slander uttered need not be something utterly false, but a true statement maliciously uttered to hurt another's reputation. In the letter to the Colossians (3:8) *malice* and *slander* are mentioned again in condemnation.

In the matter of confessing and making amends for unkind criticism, a person convicted requires tact as well as frankness. If a Christian has made a hurtful statement about another Christian to a third party, the third party should be informed that the statement made was false or malicious. The second person, the offended one, may not have heard the criticism, and so it is not always necessary to confess the details of the criticism to him, for fear of unnecessarily wounding his feelings—only the spirit of criticism should be confessed in this case. Likewise, in making open confession of a spirit of criticism care should be taken not to give wider currency to the malicious statement. It behoves every convicted Christian to pray for wisdom in making restitution of wrongs.

Levity

In the Ephesian Letter (5:4) the Apostle Paul warns against *levity* which is defined as unseemly frivolity or jocularity, as well as silly talk which, in the Greek original, suggests "talking like a moron". Robertson distinguishes between *nimbleness of repartee* on the one hand and *ribaldry* on the other. The distinction in the Greek is worth making in the English, for there is all the difference in the world between a sense of humour and foolish jesting.

Bishop Taylor Smith used to pray: "Grant unto us, O Lord, the saving grace of a sense of humour!" Humour is a saving grace, for it comes from a correct sense of perspective. People with a kindly sense of humour are never arrogant or proud or spiteful. They more often depreciate themselves than others. Humour is the salt which helps us masticate the tough fare of life. Humour cheers up others in trouble.

Jesting, on the other hand, is not fitting. It consists in making jokes or thrusts at the expense of others. It is generally vulgar. It is the enemy of serious conversation. It achieves nothing. It should be avoided no matter what the example may be. Humour may help at a Christian banquet or youth rally; jesting sets the meeting back.

Grumbling

Nearly every church has a grumbler, to whom nothing seems right. He grumbles at everything under the sun. He is the despair of his friends. Grumbling is a sin of the tongue, a habit pattern which betrays a spiritual condition. A Christian full of love, joy, and peace does not grumble, even though he may be enduring heavy trials. The grumbler is in rebellion, not against petty circumstances, but against God. The Apostle Paul exhorted the Philippian believers (2:14) to "do all things without grumbling or questioning!" The first dispute in the Christian Church came about through grumbling

(Acts 6:1) and the bad business has been going on ever since. The cure for grumbling is prayer and praise, which go in pairs.

Foul Talk

Impure conversation is the deadly enemy of spirituality. This *foul talk* is condemned in the Ephesian Letter (4:29, 5:3-4, 5:12) but as it is part of the larger subject of impurity of thought, word and deed, it will be treated in another section.

CHAPTER SIX

SINS OF UNCHASTITY

IN THE Scriptures, no other sin is mentioned more often with disapproval and threats than unchastity, or carnal vice in its various forms, for no other sin is more widespread and natural than sex sin. There appears to be no other area of human life in which wickedness has wreaked more havoc than in sexual relations.

Among Christians, discussion of impurity is deemed distasteful. If unchastity reared its ugly head only among unbelievers, this Victorian taboo would make sense. But what pastor or teacher or evangelist or chaplain would deny that unchastity is a major threat to the believer in his Christian life? Between the Victorian conspiracy of silence on the subject and the modern racket of loquacity, the Christian has a middle course already prepared for him, to teach the precepts of Scripture in the language, emphasis and balance of Scripture.

General Counsel

There is something different about the sin of immorality. A man may lie, but may apologise. A man may steal, but may make restitution. But an immoral man sins against his personality. Five minutes of foolishness may result in the ruin of a character, havoc of a home, hurt of a family, damage of a church.

The Apostle Paul counselled the careless Corinthians:

"Shun immorality. Every other sin which a man commits is outside the body; but the immoral man sins against his own body. Do you not know that your body is a temple of the Holy Spirit within you, which you have from God? You are not your own; you were bought with a price. So glorify God in your body" (1 Corinthians 6:18–20).

In this passage, the main idea in the mind of the Apostle Paul is that immorality (fornication, in a general sense, to King James translators) breaks the spiritual bond between the body and Christ and makes the body itself the instrument of sin in a way not true of other dreadful sins. Such immorality is capable of blighting the body with horrible diseases, and, worse again, of cursing unborn children in the same way. Immorality is a deadly vice.

Thought

In the antediluvian days of deterioration, God saw that the wickedness of man was great upon the earth, and that every imagination of the thoughts of his heart was only evil continually. Human nature has not changed, and as a man thinketh in his heart today, so is he. In the words of Christ (Mark 7:21-22): "Out of the heart of man come evil thoughts...fornication...adultery...licentiousness... an evil eye..."

Most temptations to impurity in the imagination are visual. It was so with Potiphar's wife, with Samson, with King David, and the righteous Job found it necessary to say (Job 31:1): "I made a covenant with mine eyes; why then should I think upon a maid?" The Master said clearly (Matthew 5:28): "Every one who looks at a woman lustfully has already committed adultery with her in his heart." And the Apostle Peter denounced those (2 Peter 2:14) who had "eyes full of adultery, insatiable for sin".

The Christian should protect his eyes. He should avoid company which is provocative. Most of all, he should guard his mind in times of relaxation, remembering that it is always dangerous to give way to thoughts of sex indulgence when they are impossible of legitimate fulfilment in marriage. The unmarried should always avoid mental indulgence, and the married should avoid thought of even legitimate indulgence when such occur in the absence of the married partner, for in one case there comes a temptation to fornication and in the other to adultery, in the modern sense of those terms.

Purity of thought is the first line of defence for the Christian. One who is pure in thought is seldom caught unaware by temptation to impurity of action. "Each person is tempted when he is lured and enticed by his own desire. Then desire when it has conceived gives birth to sin; and sin when it is full-grown brings forth death" (James 1:14-15).

Words

Most Christians instinctively shrink from impurity of conversation. Thoughts with which they flirt in the hidden chambers of the mind are not permitted to expose themselves to the critical ear of other Christians. Yet, in practice, many Christians have intimate friends with whom they lower the barriers to improper conversation.

"Let no evil talk come out of your mouths," wrote the Apostle Paul (Ephesians 4:29, 5:4); "let there be no filthiness." Sex should be treated as a sacred subject, never a sport.

It is wise for the Christian to avoid discussing the scandals of the wicked, for the very discussion of them conjures up defiling mental images. It is a shame even to speak of the things they do in secret (Ephesians 5:12). Many a chaplain would give a lot to be able to forget what he had to hear.

Christian girls would do well to avoid discussion of sex with eligible young men. There is a loss of modesty involved. In the world, seducers brag of their progress from mundane conversation to dangerous subjects. Even with men who have no thought of seduction, a too frank discussion of sex with an eligible girl becomes a temptation. One would not recommend frank discussion of marital matters with even a lover until the wedding day has been fixed, and the discussion should then be a common sense planning of married life, not a mental anticipation of pleasures forbidden until the union is sanctified by marriage.

In modern educational procedures, a certain amount of co-educational discussion of sex in scientific terms becomes inevitable. The Christian student will let the discussion end in the classroom, so far as the opposite sex is concerned. It is permissible to condemn by scriptural word and godly counsel all impurity presented in conversation.

Deeds

The natural outcome of undisciplined thought is undisciplined action. Among the adolescent, and also among those who remain adolescent in their attitudes, solitary impurity is a sad but widespread practice, one which is far too often a problem among professing Christians who have never been clearly taught.

The modern fashion is to excuse such bad habits as mere immaturities. The non-Christian psychiatrist seeks to remove the feeling of guilt from the weakling. Comparisons are made with lower animals, statistics are quoted, but they do not make right what is wrong.

In 1937, in Britain, I drove an Armstrong-Siddeley car which had an unusual brass self-starter ring which made a pleasing tinkle as it engaged the fly-wheel. Sometimes, trying to enliven the conversation with *sassenach* passengers, I would punch the horn-button of the car to make it emit a cheerful *honk-tiddly-honk-honk—ching-ching*, the last two notes being derived from pressing the self-starter button with its brass effect. That I was wreaking damage upon the brass self-starter ring did not occur to me. The self-starter button was meant for pushing, I would have said. But a motor mechanic showed me that the brass teeth of the self-starter ring were being worn off by being thrown against the steel fly-wheel in the wrong circumstances, when it was revving hard. The self-starter button was designed for pushing in restricted circumstances. Likewise, the procreative apparatus in man was designed by the Creator for use in prescribed circumstances, sanctified by marriage. All other use is therefore abuse, and brings about damage in the physical, mental and spiritual realms, as I learned in counsel in the chaplaincy.

The Psalmist prayed to be delivered from "secret faults" and "secret sins". It takes the light of God to deliver sinners from "what they do in the dark, every man in the chambers of his imagery".

The word *fornication* is mentioned in condemnation in a dozen books of the Bible, but is seldom mentioned in Christian preaching and teaching, chiefly because it is distasteful. In the Scriptures, the word is used in at least three ways:

figuratively, to describe idolatry which is regarded as infidelity to God and intercourse with wickedness; *generally*, to describe all immorality, by which word the modern translators give that sense; and *particularly*, to describe illicit sexual intercourse on the part of an unmarried person, which is the modern usage defined in the dictionary.

The Scripture is explicit. The Phillips translation of the New Testament Epistles, *Letters to Young Churches*, gives in cursive style the sense of 1 Corinthians 7:1-2 thus:

> "It is a good principle for a man to have no physical contact with women. Nevertheless, because casual liaisons are so prevalent, let every man have his own wife and every woman her own husband."

Unmarried people are not permitted to indulge in sexual relationship under any excuse. The average Christian is aware of the impropriety of casual relationships. Most young people face temptation in steady courtship, and are sometimes willing to consider increasing intimacy as permissible on account of their genuine love and honest intentions. This is a snare. "If they cannot exercise self-control, they should marry. For it is better to marry than to be aflame with passion" (1 Corinthians 7:9).

The answer to the problem of the strain of courtship is marriage. There is no answer to the problem of casual liaison and prostitution except to abstain utterly. Such fornication is wickedness. Every Christian ought to know this, and yet one knows of so-called Christians who think that illicit liaisons are permissible so long as precautions are taken. The First Corinthian Letter teaches clearly that Christians are not to associate, not even to sit at table, with an admitted fornicator who claims that he is a Christian.

Adultery is defined in the dictionary as voluntary sexual intercourse by a married man with another than his wife, or by a married woman with another than her husband. In Scripture, *adultery* designates sexual intercourse of a man, whether married or unmarried, with the wife of another man. Adultery in both dictionary and scripture signifies a breach of the integrity of the family unit, which God established as a sacred institution in society.

The Seventh Commandment categorically prohibited adultery, and the law prescribed the death penalty for both adulterer and adulteress. Job characterized it as a heinous crime (Job 31:11). The Old Testament prophets condemned adultery, and the New Testament reiterated the condemnation.

Marriage is so established in mutual love that the problem of adultery should not arise for any Christian couple. Both husband and wife should see to it that the mutual love is established and maintained in every way, spiritual, mental and physical. Alas, it is a deplorable fact that the majority of marriages of Christian people are not completely mutual. There is something wrong if the sacred relationship in its physical aspects should mean pleasure for one and anything less for the other. The ignorance of some Christians on the subject is appalling. The solution to so many problems is simple.

There are worse offences than fornication or adultery, but the very contemplation of perversion is defiling. Sinners who carry their rebellion against God as far as promiscuity are often tempted to go further into unnatural things, as in Romans 1:26-27:

"For this reason God gave them up to dishonourable passions. Their women exchanged natural relations for unnatural, and the men likewise..."

For any one to name the name of Christ and fall into such wickedness seems almost incredible, and yet it has been known. The judgment of God falls upon all who sin so.

CHAPTER SEVEN

SINS OF WRONGFUL POSSESSION

T HERE is nothing more explicit in the Decalogue than the commandment, "Thou shalt not steal!" In the chaplaincy, one found that the commandment against stealing was the easiest to quote to show that the laws of God are not based upon the arbitrary whim of a Supreme Being unrelated to the good of the human race, which good is the will of God. It was easy to picture the chaos which would result from a wholesale departure from the commandment against stealing.

Stealing

In times of the moving of the Holy Spirit, professing Christians are often known to confess outright stealing. There is only one thing to do in such a case: to confess the theft to the person wronged and to offer to make restitution; and if restitution is beyond the power of the individual, he ought to throw himself upon the mercy of the person or persons from whom he stole.

I have heard it said that it is superfluous to warn Christians against stealing, seeing that Christians cannot steal and still be Christians! There is only one reply to that: both the Apostle Paul and the Apostle Peter warned Christians against stealing, the former saying (Ephesians 4:28): "Let the thief no longer steal, but rather let him labour, doing honest work with his hands, so that he may be able to give to those in need," and the latter urging that no Christian should suffer as a thief (1 Peter 4:15).

Pilfering

As in the matter of lying, Christians find their consciences too tender for outright stealing, but often give way to some act they consider short of it. They pilfer little things, they misappropriate; they take what they consider unimportant things without permission. The Apostle Paul warns all Christian employees (or servants) not to pilfer, but to show entire and true fidelity (Titus 2:10).

It was said that, during the Nicholson Awakening in Northern Ireland in the 1920s, so many shipyard workers came under conviction of the sin of pilfering tools and began returning them, the management posted notices giving blanket forgiveness to all offenders but asking them to keep the stolen tools on account of the sudden overcrowding of tool sheds! A student at a college in the Pacific Northwest approached me about the matter of pilfering, and, when questions were asked, it appeared that he had "pilfered" a motorboat of considerable size! Sometimes I have found Christians half-convicted about the pilfering of little things like postage stamps and telephone calls which are charged to the firm. There is a simple test. If the employer agrees that the privileges of the employee include free stamps and telephone calls, by all means the Christian ought to take advantage of such generosity.

Stealing is stealing no matter how one may rationalize. In several revival campaigns, I have been approached by professing Christians who had become convicted of the pilfering of small sums of money from their employers, and, in each case, the excuse was the complaint that the employer had not been paying high enough wages. Alas for the excuse, the employer must be the judge of that, or, if he actually cheats the employee must appeal to the law, not to private readjustment!

I have been asked hypothetical questions about stealing under circumstances of extreme necessity, such as a mountaineer with a broken leg, starving to death, dragging himself to a cabin which is well-stocked with food but with the owner away. I personally would have no compunction in such circumstances immediately to put into operation the principle involved in Deuteronomy 23:24, offering to make good on the first opportunity. I suspect that the people so interested in such hypothetical emergencies are often more concerned with conscience easing in the matter of another more complicated misappropriation.

The Scripture is explicit regarding the sin of misappropriation by an *employee*: it is equally implicit about defrauding by *employers*. The first six verses of James 5 constitute as strong an indictment of social injustice as any in literature. It is a sin for an employer not to pay a hired man a living wage (Malachi 3:5), or to withhold wages by fraud (James 5:4), or to delay the payment of wages (Deuteronomy 24:15), or to use a neighbour's service without wages (Jeremiah 22:13), or to be inconsiderate of employees' complaints (Job 31:13). I wish I could say that such injustices were unknown among Christian employers. Nevertheless, there have been Christian employers in all ages who had a passion for social justice. Social justice was also the passion for six humble workers, known in trade-union history as the Tolpuddle Martyrs, transported to the convict camps of Australia for forming a trade union to contest an employers' agreement to keep wages at seven shillings (one dollar) a week... five of these pioneers of trade unions were local preachers or Christian workers, and the sixth was converted through their Christian witness in the labour gangs. Lord Shaftesbury, an aristocrat but a Christian, was England's greatest social reformer; and Keir Hardie, a coal miner but a Christian convert of Moody, was Britain's greatest advocate of the rights of the working man, writing his first tract on Proverbs 30:8, entitled *Can a man be a Christian on a Pound a Week?*

Unpaid Debts

Stealing may manifest itself in the matter of unpaid debts. A Christian is under obligation to pay back what he has borrowed, for it is a wicked thing to borrow and not pay again (Psalm 37:21). Business investment should be distinguished from borrowing (in which the borrower has all the advantage), for an investor agrees to let a businessman use his money in a calculated risk. The Christian businessman will try to return both capital and interest to the investor, but there are circumstances where business failure should be borne and shared by all who had hoped to gain a profit from the business.

It appears from the Scriptures that debts are not to be repudiated (2 Kings 4:7). The Apostle Paul advises Christians to be in debt to no one (Romans 13:8). In view of the modern business practice of credit-buying, it should be pointed out that the sort of debt which the Scriptures condemn is neglect of meeting payment on just contracts. If a man lend a friend a sum of money for a year, or until a certain date or circumstance in which repayment is expected, the debtor is not guilty of breaking his contract until the repayment falls due. In America, it appears that most of the population purchase goods on the instalment plan. The purchaser herein makes a contract with the good will of the seller, and, providing he meets his instalments promptly, he has not broken a contract. It is, of course, very unwise to purchase more than one's income can meet: but, even so, the purchaser may still salve his conscience by returning the goods, whose good condition is generally and wisely safeguarded by insurance.

I was once speaking in a London college when a big Irishman arose to demand: "D'you mean that a fella has to pay back all the debts he made before his conversion?" Thinking of the principle involved in the case of Zacchaeus, I answered in the affirmative. "Then," said he in disgust, "I'll be workin' from now till the Millennium and right through the Thousand Years!" Not wanting to rob him of the prospect of working a little for the Lord during that lengthy period, I inquired the nature of the debts. They were gambling debts, he said. He was reassured when I gave my opinion that a gambling debt was illegal and not binding. Anyone with any doubts about this should reflect that the first thing that a bookie does to collect one of his unenforceable payments is to persuade, sometimes under threat of violence, the debtor to sign a chit for a legally enforceable contract to pay.

Business Integrity

The Scripture is very clear also concerning sharp business practice, between buyer and seller. "A false balance is abomination to the Lord: but a just weight is his delight" (Proverbs 11:1). It is therefore very wrong for a Christian salesman to misrepresent the value of goods to a buyer. Proverbs 21:6 condemns the making of profits by misrepresentation, and, according to Deuteronomy

25:13-16, it is unjust to have double standards in business.

There remains the question of indebtedness to established authorities, about which the Apostle Paul wrote to the Roman Christians (13:6-7):

> "For the same reason you also pay taxes, for the authorities are ministers of God, attending to this very thing. Pay all of them their dues, taxes to whom taxes are due, revenue to whom revenue is due, respect to whom respect is due, honour to whom honour is due."

It is noteworthy that every great revival of true religion sends conscience money to tax collectors from offenders convicted through the preaching of the Word or the operation of the Spirit.

It is certainly our conclusion that a Christian who has enjoyed the use of possession of another person's money or property unlawfully cannot enjoy the blessing of God at the same time. Property rights under law are ordained of God, and transgression of them is an offence against Him.

Robbing God

There is a more direct offence against God: in the words of Malachi 3:8-10:

> "Will a man rob God? Yet ye have robbed Me. But ye say, Wherein have we robbed Thee? In tithes and offerings! Ye are cursed with a curse: for ye have robbed Me, even this whole nation. Bring ye all the tithes into the storehouse, that there may be meat in my house, and prove Me now herewith, saith the Lord of hosts, if I will not open you the windows of heaven, and pour you out a blessing, that there shall not be room enough to receive it."

To steal from a bank is bad enough: to steal from a benefactor is worse. Yet that is what so many believers do. By withholding their tithes and offerings, they rob God. Some avoid conviction by contending that tithing is Old Testament Law not binding on the Church today. One can only reply that, if a Jew under the Law was obliged to give his tenth, a Christian under Grace should do better than that.

Some Christians say, at the end of the week (or month), "I do not have it to give." The Scripture teaches that we should lay aside our contribution at the beginning of the week. Too many believers are like the little girl who, given a penny for the Lord's work in the Sunday School and another for herself, tripped and fell, recovered one penny and put it in her pocket, lost the other down a drain, then exclaimed: "O Lord, there goes your penny!"

CHAPTER EIGHT

SINS OF THE SPIRIT

MOST Christians are startled when they learn that the sins of the spirit are a far greater hindrance to spiritual revival than the sins of the flesh. This contrast can be seen in the attitude of our Lord, who was doubly lenient with the woman taken in adultery, and trebly severe with the pride of the Pharisee. This does not mean that adultery is less culpable than pride, but rather that one who gives way to pride is harder to help than one who gives way to adultery.

Pride

God resists the proud, but gives grace to the humble (1 Peter 5:5). The first sin of Satan, the angelic being created perfect, was pride, which was the iniquity found in him. (Cf. Ezekiel 28:15 *ff.* and Isaiah 14:12 *ff.*) His ego, inflated with sacrilegious pride, asserted itself in a five-fold defiance of God: "I will...I will...I will...I will...I will...!"

The heart of pride is egotism, self-centredness. The self-centred man is really eccentric, coming into collision with everything moving. The humble man is God-centred, and so finds his orbit in proper relationship with the orbits of all other men so God-centred.

Pride is a high esteem of oneself for one's talents, achievements, merits or position. The humble man is not unaware of privilege of talents, achievements, merits or position, but ascribes them to God and submits them to God's purpose.

Vanity is empty or mistaken pride in imagined attainments, together with a desire for the notice, approval or praise of others. The humble Christian is not without a desire for notice, approval or praise, but he seeks first the notice and approval and praise of God, and abhors the praise of men when it is in conflict with the approbation of God.

Conceit is vanity added to pride, and it is so supercilious that it thrives upon the depreciation of others.

There is another type of pride, inverted pride, commoner in England than in America, in which one takes pride in not appearing to be proud. Cultivated self-depreciation if undertaken with a view to the approval of others, is just as deplorable as bragging. In fact, it is hypocritical humility. I knew a man in Oxford University who unwittingly *bragged* that, although he had just as much to be proud of as any American, he refrained from bragging. A humble man is not a man who keeps his pride bound and gagged in company, but gives it an airing privately: he seeks to crucify his pride.

Hypocrisy

Hypocrisy is a spiritual sin for which Christ reserved His strongest condemnation. He had little patience with the Pharisees, telling them (Matthew 23:28): "So you also outwardly appear righteous to men, but within you are full of hypocrisy and iniquity." Hypocrisy is nothing more than pretence, playing a part which is not in keeping with the truth. The Pharisees were concerned with the minor details of the Law, but neglected the weightier matters such as justice and mercy and faith. Any Christian who strikes a spiritual pose and does not live up to it is a hypocrite.

Neglect of Prayer

Prayerlessness is another sin of omission. It is a sort of creeping paralysis, which begins in neglect of prayer and ends in utter prayerlessness. Prayerlessness is the root sin. By neglect of prayer, a Christian becomes prey to a hundred vices. All sorts of creeping things crawl underneath the heavy stone of neglect, which once removed causes them to scurry out of the sunshine of fellowship with God. By neglecting prayer, a Christian robs himself of the counsel of God, quenches the Spirit, hinders his growth in Christ. He finds it easier in prayerlessness to harden his heart against his brother and his neighbour. The only cure for prayerlessness is prayer. Such prayer should begin with the confession of the sin of prayerlessness. If the prayerless one still finds it hard to pray, then he should start to praise God for his many wonderful benefits. If praise does not loosen his tongue, then he should confess the sin of ingratitude.

Neglect of Devotions

In confessing prayerlessness, the Christian should remember that lack of intercession for others to whom it is promised is also sin. Samuel the prophet said: "God forbid that I should sin against the Lord in ceasing to pray for you." A Christian should be especially careful about keeping his promises of intercession to missionaries.

It is impossible for one Christian to prescribe a programme of prayer for another Christian. It is impossible for a Christian to prescribe a programme of prayer for himself. Prayer is devotion to God. Just as an affectionate husband does not tell himself, "I must set aside fifteen minutes each day for kind words with my wife!" so a Christian cannot allot his time to God. The loving husband gives all the time that he can to his wife; and the faithful Christian turns his thoughts to God every time they are not necessarily preoccupied with something else. As the negroes sing in their Spiritual: "Every time I feel the Spirit moving in my heart, I will pray!"

The best plan for prayer is that of the Psalmist, who prayed every evening, morning and at noon. Bedtime is not the best time for prayer. The best times are before the responsibilities of the morning, afternoon, and evening. But, along with regular recourse to prayer, the believer should be ready to turn to God every time a decision is to be made, a contact to be exploited for Christ, a temptation to be resisted; in fact every possible moment which can be devoted to contact with God should be given to prayer.

Devotional reading is likewise neglected by too many Christians. It is often more important to begin by reading the Word than to pray first. It is more important that the Holy Spirit should have the opportunity of speaking to us through the Word than that we should unburden ourselves of our habitual expressions. The Lord can care for us without our telling Him, but we cannot obey His voice without hearing it.

Bible study should not be made to do duty for devotional reading. Any reading of the Scriptures necessary for the proper preparation of a sermon or lecture or talk should be treated as part of that service, and not allowed to crowd out devotional reading needed for the nourishment of one's own soul. The reading of doctrinal matter in which one has a hobby interest should be avoided in the quiet time.

Neglect of family reading is a common temptation of Christians. Life is so crowded that opportunities for corporate family worship are few. The Christian family which prays together, stays together.

Neglect of Witness

Neglect of witness, better called cowardice or indifference, is another besetting sin of spiritual Christians. They give lip assent to the need of witness, but seldom do anything about it. They rescue the perishing occasionally in stirring stanzas of hopeful hymns, but they do not put their sentiments into practice in real life outside the church building. Christians find it easier to talk about the weather, business, family, politics, sports or almost anything but Christ Himself. This is a sin.

Lovelessness

Lovelessness is the cause of neglect of prayer, devotional reading and soulwinning. Lovelessness is the greatest sin of all, for Christ Himself tells us that the first and greatest commandment is, "You shall love the Lord your God with all your heart, and with all your soul, and with all your mind and with all your strength" (Mark 12:30), so transgression of the first and greatest commandment constitutes the first and greatest sin.

Unbelief

Unbelief is the final sin. A Christian may repent of his pride, hypocrisy, prayerlessness, neglect of reading, cowardice, and lovelessness; but if he is unbelieving and hard in heart, the Lord can do nothing for him. Christ was unable to do many mighty works because of the unbelief of His fellow citizens in Galilee. The writer of the Epistle to the Hebrews (3:12) names *unbelief* as the beginning of backsliding in the warning: "Take care, brethren, lest there be in any of you an evil, unbelieving heart, leading you to fall away from the living God."

Our salvation is by faith. By faith comes every subsequent blessing, whether of repentance, or confession, or forgiveness, or cleansing, or victory, or surrender, or filling, or call, or service. It is by faith that we walk, and unbelief is departure from the walk of faith. Whether it exists as petty worry, or occasional doubt, or continued unbelief, it is *not of faith,* and whatever is *not of faith* is sin (Romans 14:23).

It is impossible to exaggerate the importance of faith in the very Word of God. Feeling follows faith, and faith follows fact, and the facts are contained in the Word of God.

CHAPTER NINE

THE CLEANSING OF THE CHRISTIAN

IN THE inquiry room of an evangelistic campaign recently, I heard a zealous Christian worker tell an unconverted man that his sins could be forgiven and cleansed if he would only confess them. The worker assured him that the Scripture said so in 1 John 1:9: "If we confess our sins, He is faithful and just and will forgive our sins and cleanse us from all unrighteousness."

This is a very common misapplication of a familiar promise to believers. No one can promise cleansing through confession to an unregenerate man. No one has the right to tell a gangster that, if he takes a full-page advertisement in the city papers to confess his sins against society, he will automatically receive cleansing from God. God requires the unconverted man to repent and become converted and receive the Lord Jesus Christ as his Saviour.

The word *cleansing* (*katharsis*) in its various forms is translated as *clean, cleanse, prune, purge, purify*, etc., in the New Testament, meaning either physical, medical, legal, ceremonial or spiritual cleansing. It is a striking fact that the subjects of spiritual cleansing are always believers in Christ. The doctrine of *katharsis* is a doctrine of the purification of saints, not of the justification of sinners. It is true that the repentant sinner, upon acceptance of Christ, is justified, and then he enjoys the premier cleansing of the Blood of Christ, by the Word of God. But no unjustified man is cleansed. Cleansing is for Christians.

Christ's conversation with Peter (John 13:3-11) showed that the disciples had been laved (cleansed wholly) by the Word, but still needed the washing of the feet. The cleansing of the Blood of Christ is continuous.* Both the initial cleansing and the periodic cleansing are for Christians.

There is a difference between forgiveness and cleansing. Hitherto, I had always regarded the promises of 1 John 1:9, "He will forgive us our sins and cleanse us from all unrighteousness", as two ways of describing the same blessing. But I have come to see that two different things are promised therein. The things that are forgiven are "sins", acts of sin, specific sins; the thing that is cleansed is the whole personality, cleansed from *all* unrighteousness.

My small boy, David, was once told not to play in a tempting mud puddle. He disobeyed. To his dismay, he discovered that the muddy evidence of his disobedience was written all over his face and hands and knees and clothes. Fearing just punishment, he stayed out late, until the twin forces of fear of the dark and miserable hunger drove him in. By this time, we were so relieved to see him that we forgave him promptly. But as soon as he was forgiven, his mother took him to the bathroom, and stripped off his dirty clothes, washed his dirty face and hands and knees, and then put him into the tub for a complete bath, finally deciding to give him a shampoo. So he went to bed, not only forgiven of his disobedience, but as clean as a new pin.

A friend of mine left his car in the garage to

*Linear as well as punctiliar, as demonstrated by the Greek tense used in 1 John 1:7.

be checked for a speck of dirt in the carburettor. The mechanic discovered that not only was the carburettor dirty but the car required new spark plugs, new distributor points, new radiator hose, new rear tires and a wax job. So what began as a minor adjustment ended in a happy overhaul.

I cannot forget the testimony of a young lady in a Minnesota college soon after the school had been moved to seek forgiveness. "I want to thank God," she said, "for loving me enough to want to clean me up after all this mess I have been in." That has been typical of the college revivals known to me. The misery of painful confession and reconciliation has always been followed by a period of cleansing so convincing to the students that the campus has been swept by infectious praise.

It is not enough to preach the Word until Christians are convicted, are confessing or are forgiven. They must be urged to accept by faith the general cleansing of the personality which God happily performs following the humbling over some specific matter.

In the Old Testament, there is a story which illustrates the difference between forgiveness and cleansing. The fifty-first psalm was written after David, a man of God, had sinned grievously. Nathan the prophet had told the King that he was guilty, and David readily admitted his guilt, saying: "I have sinned against the Lord!" Thereupon, Nathan had told David that the Lord had put away his sin. His sin was forgiven.

Did David believe the promise of God in the words of Nathan? Did he still cry for forgiveness of adultery and murder? Psalm 51 was written the day that Nathan had rebuked David for his sin. In its heartfelt petitions there is no request for forgiveness, but there are many requests for cleansing. David had gained a glimpse of the uncleanness of his heart: hence his prayers were for the blotting out of his many transgressions, the washing thoroughly from all his iniquities, the cleansing from his sin. He asked the Lord to purge him as with a broom, to wash him whiter than snow.

"Create in me a clean heart, O God, and renew a right spirit within me!" That was not a prayer for forgiveness, for David had been told that his sin had been forgiven when he had confessed it. It was a prayer for cleansing.

In the New Testament, the Christian is told that if he confessed his sins, God is faithful and just to forgive him his sins, and to cleanse him from *all* unrighteousness. This wording is not accidental. Many a time, a Christian has become deeply convicted of some particular sin, and has at last confessed it, seeking forgiveness; but with the forgiveness of the particular sin has come a realization of his need of cleansing from inward sin, from all unrighteousness. The cleansing covers a larger area than the original area of conviction.

During the striking revival at Ngaruawahia in New Zealand in 1936 (described by Oswald Sanders in *The Reaper*), I was led to write the words of the prayer-hymn set to the tune of the old Maori folk-song *Po ata rau—Now is the Hour*:

> *Search me, O God, and know my heart today,*
> > *Try me, O Saviour, know my thoughts, I pray:*
> *See if there be some wicked way in me:*
> > *Cleanse me from every sin and set me free.*
>
> *I pray Thee, Lord, to cleanse me now from sin:*
> > *Fulfil Thy promise: make me pure within:*
> *Fill me with fire where once I burned with shame:*
> > *Grant my desire to magnify Thy name.*

Lord, take my life and make it all Thine own:
I want to spend it serving Thee alone:
Take all my will, my passion, self and pride—
I now surrender, Lord, in me abide.

O Holy Ghost, revival comes from Thee!
Send a revival, start the work in me!
Thy Word declares Thou wilt supply our need—
For blessing now, O Lord, I humbly plead.

CHAPTER TEN

SANCTIFICATION THREEFOLD

SALVATION has a threefold effect: the effect of Justification is to deliver the believer from the guilt of sin; the effect of Sanctification is to deliver the believer from the power of sin; and the effect of Glorification is to deliver the believer from the presence of sin.

When a man accepts Jesus Christ as Saviour by faith, he is delivered from the guilt of sin; when he meets Jesus Christ face to face in death or rapture, he is delivered from the presence of sin; but between these two events he lives his life on earth in which the indwelling Holy Spirit seeks to deliver him from the power of sin.

There has been so much controversy about Sanctification that the average Christian leaves the subject severely alone, or lives in ignorance of it. And Christians who are Sanctification-conscious appear to devote their energies to debating the subject from their point of view rather than relating it to other aspects of the great truth.

There appear to be three main schools of thought regarding Sanctification. Some insist that the only holiness a believer can enjoy is that which is *positional*, or credited to him at his regeneration. Others hold that it is only by a *critical* experience that a believer can enter into a sanctified life. Others say that sanctification is *progressive*, like automatic growth in a child.

It seems to me that Scripture teaches all three views in their positive aspects, but that undue emphasis on any one of them without the balance of the other two results in a harmful heresy. It is necessary to hold the doctrine of sanctification in the same balance as taught in Scripture, which is its own best interpreter.

Let us seek to illustrate the threefold nature of Sanctification as taught in the New Testament writings. A friend of mine lost a valuable 16-mm. camera. Many months later, he discovered it in the window of a pawn shop. Upon impulse, he went into the shop and explained to the pawnbroker that the camera in the window was his. Alas, he could not give any definite proof of ownership, such as the serial number, and the pawnbroker was firm in his refusal to part with it unless the price was paid. So my friend said he would go home and get some money and redeem the camera. The pawnbroker said: "I'll set it apart for you."*

When the amateur photographer returned home with the redeemed camera, he set aside time to dust it. It worked rather unsatisfactorily, so he took it to pieces at a later date, and carefully cleaned and oiled the whole mechanism, polishing the metal and leather parts until it looked like new. Ever after that, he made it a habit to set aside the camera and devote time to keeping it in proper order and improving its operations.

It should be obvious that, in purchasing our redemption, Christ has to set us apart, first of all. In that sense, we are sanctified even before we are redeemed. Once purchased, He cleanses us from the accumulated filth of sin. Later on, as our lives are not working very satisfactorily, He gives us an overhaul. Then, as He continues to use us, He keeps

* To sanctify primarily means to set apart!

on cleansing us. Thus Sanctification is positional, critical, and progressive.

One realizes that trite illustrations sometimes blind the critical faculties of the Bible student. Too often a convenient illustration appeals to one's analytical ability. It is not enough to give illustrations unless they are illustrations of definite Scriptural statements. This illustration is certainly not without Scriptural warrant.

Positional Sanctification

For example, the Christian who insists that the holiness of Christ is posited to him at conversion has certainly the backing of Scripture for his doctrine. The First Corinthian Letter places Sanctification before Justification, and Sanctification before Redemption (6:11, 1:30). The Apostle Peter speaks in his First Letter (1:2) of the positional Sanctification of believers, and the Apostle Paul in his First Letter to the Corinthian Christians speaks of their positional Sanctification, even though the remainder of his Letter showed how far short of practical holiness they came. The Ephesian Letter (4:24) refers to the new nature of the Christian, created after the likeness of God in true righteousness and *holiness*, undoubtedly positional Sanctification. The Letter of Jude in its opening salutation alludes to the imputed Sanctification of all true believers; and so does the writer of the Letter to the Hebrews (2:11).

How can this doctrine be illustrated? I heard once somewhere of a sea tragedy in which a young fisherman was washed overboard to a watery grave. He left a young widow and a boy of eight in poverty. The good pastor who conducted the memorial service quietly opened an account in the local bank in the name of the orphaned boy, and occasionally he added to the account, which continued to bear interest. Ten years later, the boy won a scholarship in a university far to the south. The mother visited the pastor, explaining that their lack of funds prevented the boy from accepting the scholarship, for he would need a new outfit, and he would need a railway ticket for the long journey south. She was disappointed when the pastor abruptly advised her to withdraw the boy's savings from the bank. She knew of no such savings, having been able to do no more than keep up with expenses. Three weeks later, she came to see the pastor again, asking bluntly if the church could help. The pastor again told her to go to the bank and draw the savings in her boy's name. She thought it was a joke in poor taste. But, the day before the deadline, she went to the bank and discovered the unknown credit, placed there by another hand. Had her boy earned the money that he was now free to use? No, it was credited, posited. And so, at our conversion, the Lord credits to us the holiness of Christ, an inexhaustible fund of sanctification.

How, then, can this wonderful truth be twisted into a heresy? It can be made a heresy by denying the need of holy living and by ignoring the other aspects of Sanctification, critical and progressive, the practical holiness of condition rather than position.

Billy Graham was once preaching in Minneapolis on the privileges of the believer in Christ, emphasizing that God has blessed us in Christ with every spiritual blessing; with redemption, forgiveness, riches of His grace; that in Christ we are a chosen race, a royal priesthood, a holy nation, God's own people; aristocrats of heaven, ambassadors of God, servants of the Most High. An old man, sitting on a front seat, with a huge Bible under his arm, found it very exhilarating. As he pictured himself as an aristocrat of heaven, an ambassador of God, he began to interrupt the speaker with his "Amens" and "Hallelujahs", losing sight of the fact that his neighbours knew that he lived a very disappointing life. When the barrage of praise became too much for the preacher, he stopped and looked at the old Pharisee, and said: "I'm coming to you in a minute!" It is not enough to revel in positional Sanctification. If we are true believers, we are in Christ on the highest level, and the Holy Spirit is in us on our lowest level: but the purpose of the Lord is to draw us upwards in practice as well as in theory.

A Los Angeles pastor, insisting on positional Sanctification and denying critical Sanctification, unwittingly revealed this danger to me in conversation. Said he: "I had an elder in my church once, a really good Bible teacher, rightly dividing the Word of Truth, and he could smell heresy a mile away. But he had one obvious fault. He was weak regarding women, and every so often he used to run away with one of his acquaintances to the mountains, and there misbehave himself. However, he was certainly a real believer, so we just had to admit that the old nature could not be defeated!"

That same day, I heard the same pastor describing the war between the Old and New Natures, concluding that the Old Nature could not be defeated in this life. He quoted a well-known story of a Hopi Indian, giving his testimony in a meeting crowded with braves and squaws. The big man told his audience that, before his conversion, he used to go to town on Saturday night and get drunk, and then his big black dog used to bite everybody. After Jesus Christ came into his life, He gave him a great white dog, which liked to help everybody. But now the two dogs, fought against each other. A chief sitting on the front seat asked the important question: "Which dog winning?"

Said the brave, after careful reflection: "Whichever dog I feed the most!" I expected the pastor to say: "That's a picture of a carnal Christian!" Instead he said that it was the picture of a Christian until the day of his death. So I sought out the preacher, and spoke with him in this way: "There are some Christians who say that we can shoot the old black dog dead, but they agree that we can raise another black pup; so let's not bother about that. But don't you believe that it is possible to chain the old black dog up to keep him from doing damage? And don't you believe that it is possible not to *feed* the old black dog at all?"

He disagreed, saying that the old black dog could break away from any chain. I suggested that he could be put back on a chain, and starved. He disagreed. His mind was made up that little or nothing could be done with the old black dog. In his view, there did not seem to be much reliance upon the doctrine that under Grace the believer need not be under the dominion of sin.

How my friend could reconcile his view with the promise that "Sin shall not have dominion over you" I could not see. While I recognised that he himself lived a life superior to his defeatist doctrine, I could not but realise how weaker Christians could be led astray into excusing sin and confusing licence with liberty. To preach positional Sanctification to the exclusion of critical or progressive Sanctification leads to antinomianism.

Critical Sanctification

It seems to have been the experience of most deeply spiritual Christians of my acquaintance to have made definite spiritual progress immediately after conversion, in the glow of first love, and then to have leveled off or even gone down the grade until decline was recognised. The biographies of the world's greatest saints reveals much the same graph of spiritual growth. The new convert, enthused with his new experience, has not yet come to the conclusion of the Apostle Paul, "I do not understand my own actions. For I do not do what I want, but I do the very think I hate...Wretched man that I am! Who will deliver me from this body of death?"

The figure of speech—"this body of death"—is believed to have been taken from the Roman custom of chaining murderers hand and foot to the corpse of their victims. Certainly the exclamation pictures for us the disgust that a Christian, possessing the New Nature, finds in his spirit when he realises that he is dragging an odorous corpse, the Old Nature, around with him. The war between the Old and New Natures is real to every Christian as soon as he starts to grow in grace. The Apostle Paul reminded the carnal Corinthian church that they were not spiritual, but carnal Christians. The difference between a carnal and a spiritual Christian seems to lie in whether or not the believer is living a life of defeat or victory over the Old Nature.

The biographies of departed saints and the testimonies of living overcomers underline the fact that the unsatisfactory state of carnality generally provokes a crisis, whereby the believer comes to realise that God, who delivers from the guilt of sin through faith in Christ, is able to deliver the believer from the power of sin as well.

Once a student asked the evangelist whether or not he had ups and downs in his Christian life before the crisis of surrender described. The answer was in the affirmative. Whereupon the student asked if the evangelist still had ups and downs, and again the answer was yes. So the student asked: "Then what difference does it make?"

The difference, one explained, was that whereas the ups and downs of a carnal Christian are variations of a very low level of living, the ups and downs of a spiritual Christian are variations of experience on a plateau of consecration. This can be illustrated.

My wife and I once travelled from San Antonio in Texas to Mexico City. South of the muddy Rio Grande border, we found the plains of northern Mexico very dusty, dirty, hot, mosquito-infested, water-polluted and generally miserable. Up and down we went, along the dusty roads, through shabby towns, up and down but never out of the summer discomfort of the *tierra caliente* of Mexico.

At long last we reached the little town of Tamazunchale (nicknamed Thomas-and-Charlie by gringo tourists) where the road began to climb up through the mountains to the wonderful plateau of Mexico, the delightful *tierra temprada* where the air was clear, the nights cool, the mosquitoes few, the water pure, and the general conditions bracing. So we continued at an elevation of seven thousand feet, up and down but always much, much higher than the highest part of the plains, until we reached the capital city in the "Bowl of the Gods".

The Victorious Life has its ups and downs, but at an elevation far removed from the depressing ups and downs of the carnal life. There is a plateau of high and holy Christian living. "Lord, lift me up, and let me stand by faith on heaven's tableland!"

Just as a Christian who stops at positional Sanctification makes a heresy out of a blessed truth, so another who stops at critical Sanctification is guilty of a similar error. Some who rightly teach the surrender experience wrongly make it an entrance to a state of sinless perfection in which there is no further need of sanctifying grace.

Progressive Sanctification

I personally have never met anyone who lived a sinless life. I have met saints living a victorious life. I have met others who claimed to live a life free from sin, but it turned out that they meant by *sin* something short of the New Testament definition of sin. The Scriptures teach that the one who knows the right thing to do and omits doing it is guilty of sin. The Scriptures teach that whatever is not of faith is sin. Wesley calls such omissions "involuntary transgressions" rather than "wilful sin". Be that as it may, the important question is: "Are such transgressions culpable?"

A speeding driver approached a traffic signal as the yellow caution light went on, but, as he crossed the stop line, the light switched to red. Instead of braking, he coasted on over the crossing. A policeman overtook him, but he insisted that he had not driven over against the red signal. To his passenger, he explained that he had not used his accelerator to cross over; he had simply omitted to put on the brakes. He was guilty just the same.

Just as positional Sanctification is incomplete without the full surrender of the critical experience, so the crisis is incomplete without the process following. Progressive Sanctification is the experience of the believer once he has reached the higher plane.

It is not denied that a new convert grows in grace during his first love, and that an ordinary Christian makes progress in many areas of his life. But if practical Sanctification be regarded as deliverance from the power of known sin, it is apparent that only progressive Sanctification can carry on the work, so that the obedient Christian continues to walk in the light. It is the experience of Christians surrendering their lives to the Master that as soon as the light of the Spirit's operation falls upon one area, which is then cleansed, further light is given upon another area of the Christian life. The moment a believer disobeys the leading of the Spirit, he is in darkness in that respect. He does not lose his Sanctification in every area, but only in the area of disobedience, although it is too often true that the area of disobedience spreads and the believer stumbles into darkness.

Thus it is necessary to seek to live a life of progressive Sanctification. But progressive Sanctification is difficult until the surrender of critical Sanctification has been made. Some advocates of automatic progressive Sanctification are willing to accept the crisis experience as a *possible* but not *necessary* experience, saying that there are many crises of the progressive experience. It should be pointed out that, in relation to given light or known darkness, a believer is either surrendered or not surrendered. A boy of eight can fully surrender his life and enjoy the blessings of being wholly sanctified. At eighteen, sex begins to play a part in his life unknown at eight, and he must surrender that area also, which would mean another crisis. At twenty-eight, in business, his developing acquisitiveness poses him with the problem of love of money, hitherto unknown, and he must surrender that area to the Lord as well. But he cannot surrender more than 100 per cent of his life in relation to given light or known darkness. The subsequent crises at eighteen and twenty-eight do not exceed the earlier experience at eight in so far as being wholly surrendered is concerned. The lives of saints seem to show that there was a first time when they consciously yielded their all to God, and that that yieldedness was renewed from time to time.

Summary

It is surely significant that the Ephesian Letter, which declares that we are blessed with all spiritual blessings in Christ, emphatically urges the Christians to walk worthy of their calling, to add practical Sanctification to their positional blessings. It is also significant that the Roman Letter, using the aorist infinite *which is the strongest punctiliar expression,* urges believers to present as an event (not a process) their whole personalities to God as a living sacrifice, holy and acceptable; while the next verse goes on to urge them to be transformed by the renewing of their minds, all of which seems to bear out the contention made by Evan Hopkins of Keswick that practical Sanctification is a crisis with a view to a process.

CHAPTER ELEVEN

FAITH IS THE VICTORY

THE EPISTLE to the Romans, one of the greatest of all scriptural documents, was written primarily to a company of believers of above-average spirituality, as the words following the salutation indicate.

Sin

The first three chapters of the Letter to the Romans are mainly devoted to the doctrine of Sin, summed up for the reader in the well-known text: "For there is no distinction; since all have sinned and fallen short of the glory of God..." (Romans 3:23).

This insistence upon the universality of sin may be put to a test anywhere, with the same result. I once talked with a Christian Scientist who declared that Sin was simply an illusion of the mortal mind, but he admitted that he occasionally suffered from that illusion. An atheist told me that Sin was nothing more than falling short of one's own ideals, but he admitted that he fell short of his own ideals most of the time.

Justification

Just as the first three chapters deal with Sin, the next two seem to treat Justification. The first verse of the fifth chapter states: "Therefore, since we are justified by faith, we have peace with God through our Lord Jesus Christ."

The average Christian thinks of Justification as another term for forgiveness, and so misses the meaning of the great word. Some time ago, I was driving through Pasadena with Armin Gesswein, my mind more on the conversation than upon the traffic. I made what I thought was a full stop at a stop sign, and then pulled around into the boulevard crossing at right angles. A few seconds later, a traffic policeman overhauled me, insisted that I had not stopped at the intersection, but admitted that I had nearly come to a stop. As an act of grace, he forgave the offence and allowed me to proceed. I noticed in the rear-view mirror that he was still following me, so I knew that I was on probation. That was not justification.

Captain Dreyfus, an officer of the Army of France, was falsely charged and condemned to imprisonment on Devil's Island. His friends secured a retrial in which the judge exonerated the prisoner and set him at liberty. Not satisfied, Dreyfus demanded and received from the Department of War all his back pay as well as the restoration of his rank as Captain. He had been justified.

Before the First World War, a young boy at a naval academy in Britain was dismissed from the school for petty stealing. He was accused of cashing a stolen postal order, and dismissed on the testimony to the effect given by the local postmistress. Sir Edward Carson, the great British advocate, interested himself in the affair, and, although the sum involved was only five shillings (about a dollar) he proceeded to defend the lad. It was easy for Sir Edward to demonstrate that the postmistress had made the boy a victim of mistaken identity. Thus the judgment against the boy had to be revoked. But Sir Edward was not satisfied with winning the case and having the Admiralty pay the costs. He forced the Admiralty to admit the boy's legal right to be reinstated in his class. That was justification.

The important thing to notice in that key verse (Romans 5:1) is that the transition from the level of Sin to the level of Justification is by *faith*. Everyone is a sinner: that is a general conclusion. Some are justified by faith: that is a particular conclusion.

OUTLINE OF THE EPISTLE TO THE ROMANS

Section	Subject	Key Verses	Pronoun
1-3	Sin	3:23	All
4-5	Justification	5:1	We
6-7	Carnality	6:1	We
8 & 12	Spirituality	12:1-2	You
9-11	Jewish Parenthesis		
13-16	Sundry Exhortations		

Carnality

The subject of the next two chapters is the problem of carnality in the life of the Christian, posed in the opening question of the sixth chapter: "What shall we say then? Are we to continue in sin that grace may abound? By no means!" In other words, because God has been so gracious as to forgive our sins and justify us freely, are we going to show our gratitude by imposing upon His grace? God forbid. That is antinomianism.

In Soviet Russia, in the city of Leningrad, I visited the house of Prince Youssopoff, a Russian patriot who assassinated the vile monk Rasputin. Rasputin taught a particularly obnoxious form of antinomianism, to the effect that, as one who sins much must be forgiven much, the one who continues to sin with abandon enjoys more of God's forgiving grace than any ordinary sinner. Rasputin taught this evil in its most shocking form, but there are many Christians who teach it in a milder way.

The argument of the Apostle Paul may be illustrated thus. Supposing a great department store were to announce that it was prepared to forgive all outstanding debts at the beginning of the New Year, what would happen? Dishonest people, instead of being grateful for a financial gift, would rush to order more on credit, in the anticipation of running up an account which would be automatically forgiven. That sort of conversion of liberty into licence is what the Apostle condemns.

In Los Angeles, I heard a man say that, if there were two brothers, one a Christian and the other not so, and each of these brothers committed adultery, the one who was a Christian would automatically be forgiven, but that the other would go to perdition for it. That is typical antinomianism. It would be better to say that a Christian man would be unwilling to commit adultery. Living in adultery would be sufficient reason to question his status as a Christian.

So, the Apostle asks, are we going to keep on sinning in order that we may enjoy more of the forgiving grace of God? God forbid, yet it seems to be the experience of every Christian of my acquaintance that he continued to sin occasionally after his conversion to Christ. Therein lies the problem of Carnality.

Some people teach that the experience depicted for us in the seventh chapter of Romans is the life of an unconverted man. But how could an unregenerate man claim that he delighted in the law of God in his inmost self? (Romans 7:22.) Only a regenerate man could say that. The wretched man of Romans 7 appears to be the carnal Christian, defeated or still trying to live under the law.

Thus it is the carnal Christian who can say: "I do not understand my own actions, for I do not do what I want, but I do the very thing I hate" (7:15). It is sin dwelling within the Christian which brings him to despair.

It is impossible in a volume of this size to do justice to even one chapter of Romans. One must be content to deal with the highlights. In the sixth chapter of Romans one finds both a promise and a method. The promise (6:14) tells us that sin will have no dominion over us, for we are not under law but under grace. The method tells us (6:11) to reckon ourselves dead to sin and alive to God in Christ Jesus.

(a) The Promise

The words of our Saviour tell us that one who commits sin is the slave of sin. A Christian who keeps on telling lies is in bondage to lying. Through grace, that sin need not have dominion over him any more. He can break the power of deceit in his life through the grace of God. As Charles Wesley said, Christ "breaks the power of cancelled sin and sets the prisoner free".

The Law does not help us to keep the Law. The Speed Limit Warning does not help a man to keep within the Speed Limit. "Thou shalt not steal" does not prevent a man from stealing, if he so desires. But believers are not under Law but under Grace. A Russian friend of mine emigrated to the United States between World Wars. His family being poor, he was given enough money for his railway fare to Hamburg and his steamship fare to New York only. His mother provided him with a hamper full of cheese sandwiches in lieu of money for meals. By the time he reached Hamburg, he was tired of cheese sandwiches. On board ship, he could not bear the smell of good food cooking, so he retired to the top deck to eat his dry fare alone. Three days before the ship reached New York, he could bear it no more. He went to the cook and asked to be allowed to work in return for meals. For three days, he worked like a slave washing dishes for the amused cook—working like a slave and eating like a king. Only when he met his uncle in New York did he discover that his ticket included all the meals. The promise of Romans 6:14 assures believers that they need neither eat dry fare in disappointment nor work in perspiration in order to enjoy God's full provision.

(b) The Method

The exhortation "Reckon yourselves dead to sin" may be interpreted in two ways. The Calvinist may say: "God would not ask me to *reckon* myself dead if I were not actually *dead*." That seems to be a quarrel over a word. To my way of thinking, to reckon myself dead means to act as if I were dead.

In New Zealand, a young lady once approached me with a question about ballroom dancing. Now I share with Dr. Ironside the view that, if a Christian is happy and feels like dancing, there is no reason why he should not go to his room or another suitable place and dance before the Lord! But I told this young lady that I regarded ballroom dancing, like kissing games, as a mildly sexual form of entertainment not helpful to the Christian life. She asked me what I would say if someone were to ask me to go to a dance, and I enjoyed replying to her sepulchral tones: "I'm sorry. I can't dance. I'm a corpse!"

On a Pacific island, I heard a couple of soldiers urge another to join them for a night of carousing. The third fellow, a sergeant, was busy writing home, and when the others became too persuasive, he replied forcefully: "Count me out, fellows, I don't really want to go!" That was another way of saying: "Reckon me dead!"

This reckoning of oneself dead to sin and alive to God is what Matthew Henry calls mortification and vivification. One must be not only ready to act dead to sin, but act alive when the opportunity for God occurs.

Spirituality

"But," says the average Christian, "I have tried in vain to reckon myself dead to sin and alive to God. I find it difficult to live the Christian life." It is not only difficult! It is impossible to live the Christian life! Why then does God expect us to live the Christian life? Because He has made provision! Just as a sinner who cannot save himself may be saved nevertheless through the provision made in Christ, so the believer who cannot live the Christian life by himself may live victoriously through the provision God has made in the Spirit.

The eighth and twelfth chapters of Romans show that it is by the power of the Holy Spirit that we may live a victorious life. At the moment of our regeneration, we are in Christ at His high level, but at the same moment the indwelling Holy Spirit is in us at the low level of practical holiness which is the lot of every babe in Christ. It is the work of the Holy Spirit to make us more and more like Jesus Christ.

I heard the leader of a well-known American organization explain the privileges of the believer by taking his black leather-covered Testament, using it as a symbol of the blackness of the sinner's heart, and then completely enveloping it with his white handkerchief, using that as a symbol of the righteousness of Christ. The point was well made. When I asked him whether or not anything happened to the blackness of the sinner's heart in actuality under the whiteness of the Saviour's grace, he hesitated somewhat, and then said he had not thought that matter through. It needs to be examined! Practical sanctification is one of the doctrines neglected in times of no revival, or nullified by the phariseeism of extremists.

The ninth, tenth and eleventh chapters of Romans constitute the Jewish Parenthesis in which the heart of the Apostle, burdened for the salvation of his own kinsmen, breaks through the orderly array of arguments presented to the Roman Church.

In the opening verses of the twelfth chapter, he takes up again the main argument of his brief, and, indeed, comes to the climax. It is truly significant that the Apostle uses the inclusive pronoun "we" in his first argument concerning sin, his second concerning justification, his third concerning carnality, but switches to the pronoun "I" and "you" in the exhortation:

> "I appeal to you therefore, brethren, by the mercies of God, to present your bodies as a living sacrifice, holy and acceptable to God, which is your spiritual worship. Do not be conformed to this world but be transformed by the renewal of your mind, that you may prove what is the will of God, what is good and acceptable and perfect" (Romans 12:1-2).

The only possible conclusion is that the Apostle Paul had already presented his whole personality to God, but implied that the Roman Christians had not so surrendered.

However, the common interpretation of Romans 12:1 seems to make of the infinitive "to present" a sort of daily consecration of one's life to God, whereas *the Greek text makes clear that the action suggested in that case is instantaneous or punctiliar or eventual.** In other words, the verb "to present" in this case means to make a clean sweep or full surrender, and the continuing consecration is indicated in the verb "transformed" in the second verse.

The appeal, therefore, in the opening verse of Romans 12 is for a full surrender, the surrender of the intellect, will and emotions to God at a given moment rather than gradually, though the second verse urges the continual yielding of the personality day by day. The degree of yieldedness is governed by the degree of light, and the believer is expected to surrender his life to God only as he has light on the subject. Further light means further surrender, but a believer cannot surrender more than his all at any given time, therefore the first experience of full surrender is unique, often renewed but never again the same.

It may be argued, against the *crisis* significance of Romans 12:1, that the believer's life is full of crises. That is undeniable. But there must occur in the life of a believer a first time when, according to his light, he yields his life completely to God and

---

*Julius R. Mantey, Professor of New Testament at Northern Baptist Theological Seminary, co-author of the Dana & Mantey Greek Grammar, wrote the author as follows on this point: "Especially do I agree with you as to παραστησαι in Romans 12:1. A similar usage occurs in Romans 6:13 where the Apostle Paul says "Stop presenting (present imperative) your members as instruments of unrighteousness to sin, but present (aorist imperative) yourselves to God...' This single-event type of action is the distinctive contribution of the aorist tense. However, it is also used in an indefinite sense, but generally in the indicative mood...The non-indicative uses of the aorist are most often punctiliar." Dr. Mantey's comment was in reply to a question concerning his statement in the Dana & Mantey Greek Grammar (p. 190) which explained that "the aorist infinitive denotes that which is eventual or particular while the present infinitive indicates a condition or process".

finds himself proving what it is to know and follow the "good and acceptable and perfect will of God".

Full surrender, the higher Christian experience, may be nullified by sin or disobedience. It is a crisis with a view to a process, and the moment the believer resists the work of the Spirit in lifting him to still higher ground, he is in need of renewal of surrender, whether it be intellectual, volitional, or emotional in nature. However, the appeal of Romans 12:1 is for the initial yielding, and there is a truth hidden in the general outline of the Epistle concerning the method. An unbeliever proceeds from the lower level of sin to the level of Justification by *faith* and not by works: a believer proceeds from the lower level of Carnality to the level of Spirituality by *faith.*

Faith is the Victory.

CHAPTER TWELVE

THE HOLY SPIRIT

I F THE victorious life of the Christian depends
upon the Holy Spirit, it is essential that the
believer should learn something about the Holy
Spirit, who is (alas) almost unknown to many
Christians.

It is Christian doctrine that the Godhead exists
in three Persons, the Father, the Son and the Holy
Spirit. The mystery of the Trinity is something
beyond explanation, yet capable of belief. I know
that I exist as a body, as a soul, and as a spirit, and
yet I cannot say that either body or soul or spirit is
exclusively myself—I am all three. I cannot explain
this. So also, the Scriptures attribute both Deity
and Personality to the Father, the Son and the Holy
Spirit, and the Trinity is the only possible statement
of the relationship of the Persons in the Godhead, a
doctrine which is beyond all human analogy.

Personality
Christians are taught, therefore, that the
Holy Spirit is a person, and yet one often hears
presumably orthodox people refer to the Spirit as
"it" instead of "He". The Holy Spirit is someone more
than a mere influence emanating from God, and yet
that is what many Christians hold in practice if not
in theory. What do we mean by personality?

The average Christian is willing to agree to the
doctrine of the Personality of the Holy Spirit, but

seldom is able to express what he means even by
the word "person". Some say that the Holy Spirit is
an individuality, therefore a person, forgetting that
a tree can claim individuality without personality.

By personality we do not mean power. A motorist
may drive up to a service station and request the
attendant to fill his tank with the spirit of petroleum,
called gasoline in America, or petrol in Britain, or
benzine in certain other countries. The spirit of
petroleum is a dynamic power, but it has neither
mind nor will nor emotion in the matter of the use
of its power. The Holy Spirit is more than a spirit of
power from God.

The marks of personality are intellect, will, and
emotion.

A search of the Scriptures reveals that the Holy
Spirit has Intellect, Will and Emotion, the marks
of personality. For example, John 14:26: "He shall
teach you all things"—indicates that the Holy Spirit
has Intellect. Acts 16:6-7—"having been forbidden
by the Holy Spirit"—shows that the Holy Spirit
has Will. Ephesians 4:30—"Do not grieve the Holy
Spirit of God"—demonstrates that the Holy Spirit
has Emotion. God created Man in His own image,
with intellect, will and emotion, but these in Man
are limited; in God they are Infinite. The sum total
of the verses of Scripture dealing with the Holy
Spirit suggest that He is a self-conscious Being,
possessing Intellect, Will and Emotion. Many
Christians have not stopped long enough to think
this matter through to its conclusion.

(a) Intellect

If the Holy Spirit, possessing all wisdom and
knowledge, never making a mistake, is Infinite
Intellect, the sooner Christian people learn to defer
to His Superiority the better. Imagine a young

student, credited with a high intelligence quotient and excelling in high school physics, presuming to ask Professor Einstein to subordinate his greater intelligence to the lesser light of the student! Likewise, Christians must learn to subordinate their intellects to the mighty wisdom of the Spirit.

(b) Will

The same is true concerning the will. One admires the will and purpose of a man who truly triumphs over adversity by sheer effort of will. But the strongest will on earth is inferior to the Will of the Holy Spirit, whose purposes are grander infinitely than all the purposes of mankind. The Holy Spirit has been placed in charge of the work of God on earth, and He knows what He is doing, His purposes are clear, and His plans will be fulfilled.

I remember once, during the Pacific War, our outfit was ordered to pull down the mess-hall, the chapel, the briefing tents, the sleeping quarters, everything, and to pack them up and put them on board landing craft which came alongside the beach. In our excitement at the prospect of invading Japan, we did not mind living on hard rations for a while, missing our mail, sleeping out. Then came orders to take all our stuff off the ships to shore. It provoked all the grumbling of frustrated men. Cried some: "I wonder if those dopes back in Washington know how to run a war?"

But the higher command knew something that we did not know, that a plane would leave Saipan and drop a bomb on Hiroshima that week, thus bringing to a conclusion a terrible war. The higher command did not deem it wise to explain its strategic moves to tactical commanders. The converse was even more true. No private-first-class thought it his duty to plan a private campaign

against the enemy, but rather subordinated his will
to the overall purposes of the Commander-in-Chief.

So it is with the Holy Spirit. He is the
Commander-in-Chief of the Army of Christ. He is
Lord of the Harvest, supreme in revival, evangelism
and missionary endeavour. Without His consent,
other plans are bound to fail. Even now, as the
Enemy comes in like a flood, the Spirit of the Lord
lifts up a standard against him. It behoves us as
Christians to fit our tactical operations into the
plan of His strategy, which is the reviving of the
church and the evangelization of the world.

(c) Emotion

Less appreciated in the thinking of the Christian
is the Infinite Emotion of the Holy Spirit. Emotion is
a powerful force in the lives of human beings, often
surpassing intellect and will. For example, I have
a little boy in my family, and naturally I love him.
My attitude is not based on cold intellect, or grim
determination, but upon the emotion of parental
affection. It requires neither mental effort nor wilful
purpose to love my own offspring.

The Holy Spirit loves the offspring of God. This
is true of all the children of creation, but more so
does it apply to the children of God through faith
in Christ. He loves us. His love for us is a driving
force which accomplishes things for us. At the
same time, He hates sin and disobedience, and
is as ready to chasten us as a loving parent is to
discipline his child. But the emotion of the Holy
Spirit is stronger than human emotion, and is not
at all fickle. One finds that an ordinary Christian
who surrenders his life to the filling of the Spirit
is capable of loving people for whom he had not a
glimmer of love previously.

Thus it is well to consider that the Holy Spirit is a Person, with Intellect, Will and Emotion superior to our intellect, will and emotion. It is also wise to recognize that the same Scriptures which emphasize His Personality are the source of teaching concerning His Deity.

Deity

It is conceivable that a superior Being could exist with Intellect, Will and Emotion greater than ours, yet be inferior to God. How then do we know that the Holy Spirit is God?

There are references in Scripture to His creative power (e.g. Genesis 1:2: "the Spirit of God was moving over the face of the waters"). Scientists can make something from something; they have recently discovered how to make energy from matter; they may proceed to make matter from energy; but they cannot make something from nothing. That is the work of God alone. It is a power attributed to the Holy Spirit.

There are references in Scripture to His omniscience (e.g. 1 Corinthians 2:2: "For what person knows a man's thoughts except the spirit of the man which is in him? So also no one comprehends the thoughts of God except the Spirit of God"). Only God can comprehend the thoughts and wisdom of God, and this is also attributed to the Holy Spirit.

There are references in Scripture to His omnipresence (e.g. Psalm 134:7: "Whither shall I go from thy Spirit?"). Only God is omnipresent, therefore this further evidence of Deity is added to the attributes of the Holy Spirit.

There is equal rank given the Holy Spirit, with the Eternal Father and the Eternal Son (e.g. 2 Corinthians 13:14). The Scriptures also equates identity of the Holy Spirit and God (e.g. Acts 5:3-4).

There are other arguments.

Thus we have two important conclusions to reconcile: the Holy Spirit is a distinct Personality, and He is God. The doctrine of the Trinity is the only possible solution to the difficulty. It is a doctrine capable of statement and belief, but incapable of explanation.

Dr. Harry Rimmer once became involved in an argument with a Mohammedan mullah in Nigeria, the Moslem seeking to prove that Christians believe in three Gods. In reply, Dr. Rimmer asked the mullah if he possessed a living Body? A living Soul? A living Spirit? And, being answered in the affirmative and assured of the conclusions by the evidence of feeling on all three levels of existence, the evangelist asked the mullah which of the three was himself? The mullah replied "All three!" but could not explain further. Dr. Rimmer pressed home his doctrine that the Godhead, according to the Scriptures, existed in three Persons, a doctrine capable of belief but incapable of explanation.

The Lord Jesus told His disciples (John 16:7–14):

"It is to your advantage that I go away, for if I do not go away, the Counsellor will not come to you; but if I go, I will send him to you. And when he comes, he will convince the world of sin and of righteousness and of judgment: of sin, because they do not believe in me; of righteousness, because I go to the Father, and you will see me no more; of judgment, because the ruler of this world is judged. I have yet many things to say to you, but you cannot hear them now. When the Spirit of truth comes, he will guide you into all truth; for he will not speak on his own authority, but whatever he hears he will speak, and he will declare to you the things that are to come. He will glorify me, for he will take what is mine and declare it to you."

In this passage, the ministry of the Holy Spirit is announced, towards the world, towards believers, and towards the Christ.

It is significant to note His ministry towards the world, first convincing them of sin. Many people seem to think that it is the work of conscience to convince the world of sin. The popular conception of the work of conscience involves the idea: "Let your conscience be your guide!" Most people, when asked to define the work of conscience, say that the conscience tells a man what is right and what is wrong. This is an obvious fallacy, for we all know people whose consciences allow them to do things which our consciences seem to forbid. Conscience can be educated or debased. The scriptures speak of a *good* conscience, an *evil* conscience, a *pure* conscience, or a *seared* conscience in various references.

Conscience is more like an alarm clock. One may set it for 7 a.m., and it will keep ringing at 7; or one may set it at 8 a.m., and it will keep ringing at 8; or one may have occasion to rise at 6, and it will ring at 6 in the morning once its alarm hand has thus been set. I knew of a soldier overseas who assured his chaplain that his conscience would not let him drink any kind of alcoholic beverage, not even the 3.2 per cent beer supplied so freely; he drew the line at alcoholic drinks. A few months later, I saw him drinking what was obviously a can of beer, and he gave the unsolicited explanation that he now thought it quite in order to drink beer provided he refused to become intoxicated with strong drink. A few months later, I saw him drunk. He had been tampering with his conscience. Conscience is not absolute. It does not tell a man what is right and what is wrong, but rather reminds him what he believes to be right and wrong at a given time.

The Holy Spirit has absolute standards. He convinces people of sin. He uses the Word of Scripture to do so, or direct conviction, awakening the conscience. He shows the sinner the sinfulness of sin. He exposes the final sin of unbelief.

The Holy Spirit also convicts of righteousness. I heard Dr. Henrietta Mears illustrate this point to a group of young ladies. Supposing, she said, a housewife decided to spend the morning cleaning up. She soon became untidy in her personal appearance, wearing old slippers, an old overall, her face soiled by dust. At that moment, the front door bell rang, much to her dismay. There at the door was a friend from some distance away, dressed in her best clothes. It was not necessary for the visitor to point out how untidy the housewife looked. The housewife had only to look at the immaculate clothes of her visitor to realize her own shortcomings. So also the Holy Spirit presents the righteousness of Christ, which, in the days of His earthly ministry, never failed to convince men of their shortcomings.

The Holy Spirit also convicts men of judgment. It is a fact that men who have no fear of anything else tremble when the Spirit of God warns them of their fate, which is to share the eternal damnation of the prince of this world.

The Holy Spirit likewise convinces believers of carnality, sanctification, and the judgment seat of Christ. Obedient Christians, He guides into all truth. And He makes Christ, whom we have not seen, real to us, glorifying the Saviour of men in ways inexpressible but vivid.

CHAPTER THIRTEEN

THE SPIRIT AND THE BELIEVER

IN HIS conversation with Nicodemus, the Lord
Jesus referred (John 3) three times to being born
of the Spirit, identifying this regeneration by the
Spirit with being born again. It seems clear that
each true Christian is regenerated by the Holy Spirit.

In the First Letter to the Corinthians, the
Apostle Paul stated clearly that *each true Christian
is indwelt by the Holy Spirit.* The Christians to
whom he wrote (1 Corinthians 3:16) were far from
perfect, yet the Apostle told them that their bodies
were temples of the Holy Spirit.

I once stayed in a home in the Middle West, where
the family kindly made me welcome. One night, when
everyone else was out, I heard noises from upstairs.
I reassured myself that no burglars had found an
entrance, and then decided to wait until the family
returned to clear up the mystery. It seemed that the
old grandmother, of whose existence I had not heard,
was living in the attic bedroom. She was doting, so
to avoid embarrassment the family kept her out of
the way of outsiders. Nevertheless, she lived there.
Her place was recognized, but kept secret.

Too often, the neighbours of Christian people are
unaware of the indwelling of the Holy Spirit in their
lives. Christians know and recognise His place in
their lives, but not because He is an embarrassment
but because their own lives are an embarrassment,
they hide the Spirit's indwelling from the notice of

their neighbours.

The teaching of the Letter to the Romans makes clear that *each true Christian is assured by the Holy Spirit.* The Spirit Himself bears witness with our spirit that we are the children of God (Romans 8:16). This is the doctrine of the assurance of salvation, believed in ardently by Lutheran, Calvinist, Wesleyan, and every evangelical. Again, the Spirit is the witness, because the Spirit is the truth...he who believes in the Son of God has the testimony in himself (1 John 5:7, 10).

An old Scottish lady was asked how she knew she was born again, and she replied: "It is better felt than telt!" It certainly is better felt than explained. No one can tell a young man in love whether or not his love is the real thing, for only he can tell in his own soul. The assurance of salvation is a conviction wrought in the human spirit by the Spirit of God. It may be possible for a man to become a believer in Christ and suffer from a time lag in receiving the assurance of salvation, as in the case of John Wesley; but it is conversely hazardous for anyone who has no spiritual assurance of salvation to claim to be a Christian.

Each true Christian is sealed by the Holy Spirit. The Apostle Paul warned the Ephesian Christians not to grieve the Holy Spirit of God, in whom they were sealed for the day of redemption (Ephesians 4:30). In the same Letter (1:13) he specified exactly who were thus sealed: those who had heard the word of truth, the good news of their salvation, and had believed in Christ. The Corinthian Christians were told much the same thing (2 Corinthians 1:22) about the seal of the Spirit. The Greek word for *seal* is common in the Septuagint and other contemporary documents as a legal mark of ownership or closure to prevent tampering.

Each true Christian is guaranteed by the Holy Spirit, a truth taught in the same two Letters, 2 Corinthians (1:22, 5:5) and Ephesians (1:14). The Greek word for *guarantee* or *earnest* is a Phoenician business term with the same significance as the modern business term *down-payment*. The reference in Ephesians is illuminating, for it states that the promised Holy Spirit is the guarantee of our inheritance until we acquire possession of it. A further illustration of non-business nature is the engagement-ring, which is the token of marriage promised until the marriage is complete. So the Holy Spirit in our hearts is the heavenly engagement -ring, or the down-payment on the mansion in glory.

Each true Christian has been baptised by the Holy Spirit into the body of Christ. The Apostle Paul makes this doctrine clear in the First Letter to the Corinthians (12:13) and includes everyone in Christ. Baptism in water is a symbol of the baptism by the Spirit into the body of Christ. But there has been great confusion in the minds of Christians regarding this baptism by the Holy Spirit into the body of Christ, and the enduement of power or filling of the Holy Spirit, which certain Christians, with some scriptural warrant, call the *Baptism with the Spirit.**

It is clear that the reference in the First Letter to the Corinthians refers to the experience of the believer at regeneration, when by faith in Christ he receives the Holy Spirit who baptizes him into the body of Christ. Let us call that experience the Baptism *by* the Spirit. In the prediction of John the Baptist, reported by Matthew (3:2), Mark (1:8), Luke (3:16), John (1:33), fixed and dated by the ascended Christ (Acts 1:5), and referred to retrospectively by Peter (Acts 11:16), a somewhat different emphasis

*This term was so used by Finney, Booth, Moody, Torrey, Murray and other nineteenth-century leaders and did not become a subject of debate until the reaction arose against Pentecostalism.

and expression is used.

In water baptism, the agent is the minister, the subject is the believer, and the element is water. In the baptism of the believer into the body of Christ, of which water baptism is the symbol, the agent is the Spirit, the subject is the believer, and the element is Christ, for by one Spirit were we all baptised into one body. In the enduement of power, predicted by John and begun at Pentecost, the agent is Christ, the subject the believer, and the element the Spirit, reversing the order of the baptism. This shows that there is at least a case for those who refer to the enduement of power, as distinct from regeneration, as a Baptism *with* the Spirit.

It is significant, however, to note that nowhere in the Acts or Epistles, written after Pentecost, is the word *baptised with the Spirit* used to describe the experience of an individual Christian, or to urge an individual Christian to seek an enduement of power from on high. The word used in all post-Pentecostal cases concerning an individual is the word *filled* or *full*. It is true that at Pentecost, by inference, one might say that *all* the disciples were baptised by the Spirit in fulfilment of John's prediction, but the word used is *filled*. Likewise, at Caesarea, by inference, it might be said the whole company of Gentile believers were baptised with the Spirit, but the narrative does not say so directly. Throughout the Acts, the word used to describe enduement with the power of the Holy Spirit is the word *filled* or *full*, and no other words are used concerning individual believers in this connection. The exhortation of the Apostle Paul to the Ephesians (5:18) is couched in the same words: "Be filled with the Spirit!"

These observations lead me to conclude that the better term to use to describe the enduement of power is the term *filling* rather than *baptism*. Nevertheless,

I can see a connection between the two terms when used with reference to the enduement of power of the Spirit. A glass set in a sink may be quarter-filled with water, but it is not immersed. Neither can it be described as immersed when it is half full, or three-quarters full, or full to the brim. Only when the vessel is filled to overflowing is there, in the real sense of the word, an immersion or baptism. I take it that when individual Christians are filled to overflowing with the Spirit, there could be a baptism of the whole company with the Spirit. It seems to be a question of terminology, for men like Finney, Booth, Moody, Simpson and Torrey did not hesitate to use the term *baptism* for the enduement of power, whereas other great teachers like Spurgeon and Campbell Morgan preferred the term *filling*. Some good people, in their eagerness to help others into a place of power, ask the question "Have you had your baptism?"—meaning the baptism with the Spirit, not the baptism by the Spirit into Christ. This is non-scriptural phraseology. In the military forces we asked men, not "Have you had your honeymoon?", but "Are you married?" It is much better to ask a believer "Are you filled with the Holy Spirit?"—using the present tense rather than the past. It is more important to be continually filled or renewed than to be excited about a past blessing however wonderful.

To summarize these conclusions concerning a difficult subject, one which has provoked great controversy, one may say that every true Christian is regenerated, indwelt, assured, sealed, guaranteed, and baptised by the Spirit, but he may or may not be filled with the Spirit. When a seeker after Christ is born again, he is automatically regenerated, indwelt, assured, sealed, guaranteed and baptised by the Spirit. To be filled with the Spirit requires an experience of full surrender.

CHAPTER FOURTEEN

BE FILLED WITH THE SPIRIT

INTO THE heart of each obedient Christian there comes an intense yearning, not only for victory over sin, but for power for service. Christians in every generation, in every country, and in every denomination have been known to develop this desire.

The Master said: "Blessed are those who hunger and thirst for righteousness, for they shall be satisfied" (Matthew 5:6). It is inconceivable that the Lord of a perfect salvation would not make provision for every need of His children. There must be a way to purity and power.

On the last day of the feast, the Lord Jesus told the multitudes: "He who believes in Me, as the scripture has said, 'Out of his heart shall flow rivers of living water'" (John 7:38).

This is the prerogative of every Christian, but alas, how few of them avail themselves of the promise. Christians from whose inmost beings there flows a river of blessing are few and far between, yet there are enough of them to be witnesses to the truth of the enduement of power from on high.

The Lord Jesus Himself, full of the Holy Spirit, was led into the desert to face the attack of Satan at the outset of His ministry; but He returned in the power of the Spirit. These facts are recorded for us by the physician Luke, who seems to delight to record such infillings of the Spirit, both in his first treatise and in his second, which ought to be designated "*The Acts of the Holy Spirit*".

In the Acts of the Spirit, the first outpouring of the Holy Spirit occurred in the Upper Room at Pentecost, where Peter and the other ten, together with Matthias, and Mary the mother of Jesus, and the women who had followed the Lord, and a large company of disciples, about one hundred and twenty in all, were all filled with the Holy Spirit.

The effect upon Peter was startling. This disciple, who had denied His Lord with oaths and curses, stood up with the eleven and preached the first great evangelistic sermon of the Christian faith. About three thousand of the inquirers were added to the church that day. The only explanation was that the remarkable Person, the Holy Spirit, of unlimited Intellect, Will and Emotion, had taken possession of the intellect, will and emotion of Peter, using his whole personality to reach the multitudes with such convicting power that they were cut to the heart.

This incident, and indeed every other one recorded, shows that the Filling of the Holy Spirit is for service. In each instance, the infilling was followed by strong action. This was indeed the fulfilment of the promise of the Risen Christ: "You shall receive power when the Holy Spirit has come upon you" (Acts 1:8). Power for what? "You shall be my witnesses." The Filling of the Holy Spirit was not, is not, will not be given merely for spiritual ecstasy, but always for service.

But not only was the Apostle Peter filled on that glorious day of Pentecost: they were all filled, John and James and Andrew and Phillip and Thomas and Bartholomew and Matthew and James and Simon and Judas and Matthias, all apostles; also James and Joses and Judas and Simon, the brothers of

Jesus; and Mary the mother of Jesus, and Mary the mother of James and Joses, and Mary of Magdala, and Mary of Bethany, and Martha, and Joanna, and Susanna, and Salome, and other women who had been with the Lord in His ministry; a score of these who were filled are named for us, but a hundred others remain unnamed. The filling of the unnamed disciples is an encouragement indeed to every humble Christian who might be tempted to think that the power from on high is for ones whom God intends to exalt to leadership.

The Apostle Peter was filled with the Holy Spirit again, some days later. It is unwarranted to suggest that the Apostle had backslidden in the meantime. From this fact, it can be seen that the filling of the Holy Spirit has a direct relationship with immediate service. One might add, from observation, that there appear to be times of relaxation and rest in between times of enduement with power, relaxation without any grieving of the Holy Spirit. The fullness of the Holy Spirit is under the sovereignty of the Spirit rather than that of the recipient.

Another large company of Christians was filled with the Holy Spirit (Acts 4:31) and spoke the word of God with boldness. As the numbers of the believers had exceeded ten thousand, it became necessary to choose seven deacons to help the apostles in their administrations. All seven, Stephen, and Philip, and Prochorus, and Nicanor, and Timon, and Parmenas, and Nicolaus, were men full of the Holy Spirit, but the time of their initial infilling is a matter of conjecture.

The martyr Stephen, whom the evangelist Luke refers to many times as full of faith, full of grace, full of power, full of wisdom, full of the Holy Spirit, filled with the Spirit, delivered an unexcelled message of power before a hostile mob who finally stoned him to death, death overtaking him while he was yet filled with the Spirit (Acts 6:3, 5, 8, 10, 7:55).

The evangelist Philip, full of the Holy Spirit, went down to a city of Samaria, and multitudes accepted Christ. The same empowering Spirit took Philip away from the scene of his successes, down to a dirt road in the desert where he led a wayfaring Ethiopian official to Christ.

The Apostle Paul, converted as Saul of Tarsus on the road to Damascus, was visited by Ananias of Damascus that he might be filled with the Spirit. The greatest ministry of all the apostolate followed, expressed in the greatest missionary endeavour of all time. The same apostle, in Cyprus, was filled with the Spirit to discern and rebuke an evil man.

It is clear from these incidents that the filling of the Holy Spirit was given for preaching, for witnessing, for defence, for evangelism, for personal work, for missionary work, for discernment, for martyrdom.

The glorious deaths of the martyrs are inexplicable apart from the Filling of the Holy Spirit. At the beginning of the Second World War, a Korean Presbyterian pastor was seized by the Kempetai, the Nipponese Gestapo. The chief inquisitor asked him if he believed in the second coming of Jesus Christ. He said he did. He explained further that Christ would judge the world of sinners. He was asked if that included the Emperor of Nippon. Carefully paying respect to the Emperor, he said that the Emperor too would be included among the sinners unless he became a Christian. For this boldness he was beaten. The police chief asked him if he knew how Christ had died. He was crucified, said the pastor. Then, said the tormentor, that would be how the stubborn pastor would die. The Korean knew that the secret police were capable of carrying out their threats, but, instead of feeling deadly fear, he was possessed of a sudden overwhelming sense of joy that he was accounted worthy to suffer as the Saviour had suffered. Instead of crucifying him, they suspended him by the thumbs roped to a hook in the ceiling, with his arms behind his back and his toes barely grazing the ground. He was in physical agony, but his heart was filled with joy, and he was so filled with the Holy Spirit that he testified to the guards. He was finally cut down and kicked out, and certain of his flock nursed him back to health. The power of the Holy Spirit for martyrdom is still given in these days.

In the forty years of the wilderness experience between 1908 and 1948, when spiritual dearth was common, the teaching that the Filling of the Holy Spirit was only for the early apostolic days gained great popularity, but without either scriptural or historical support. In the nineteenth century, Charles G. Finney, Dwight L. Moody, William Booth, Hudson Taylor, and a host of other great leaders received the Filling of the Holy Spirit. In the twentieth century, there have been and are still great witnesses of a personal experience of the Filling of the Holy Spirit, Evan Roberts, Reuben Torrey, Wilbur Chapman, A. B. Simpson, Lionel Fletcher, and others. On the mission field, wherever there has been spiritual revival, there have been outstanding cases of the Filling of the Holy Spirit. The best and most-used Christians known to me have been men who have testified to a deeper experience of the Filling of the Holy Spirit.

Alas, in the forty years of decline, the doctrine of the Filling of the Holy Spirit has suffered not only from neglect and contradiction, but from fanatical teaching and practice. The end of the period of the nineteenth century revivals, from the Welsh Revival of 1904 to the Korean Revival of 1907, saw the rise of a great emphasis upon the work of the Spirit in what afterwards became the Pentecostal movement, whose contribution to Evangelicalism is more seriously considered today. The declining churches generally rejected the Pentecostal emphasis, driving out and persecuting its advocates. Rejected by the churches generally, the Pentecostalists were driven in upon themselves, and extreme fanaticism developed among *some* who brought discredit upon the others. Pentecostalism thrived among the less-educated classes, as happened a century earlier in Methodism; but, while many choice men of God identified themselves with the leadership of Pentecostalism there was no great scholar like John Wesley to save the movement from its friends by his insight and scholarship. Now, with the turning of the tide, it seems that the Pentecostal denominations are more and more being guided by men of moderation, and the barriers between the Pentecostal minority and the non-Pentecostal majority are being lowered, thanks not only to the decline of fanaticism among those who call themselves Pentecostalists, but also to the rising interest in the Filling of the Holy Spirit for power and gifts and fruits for service being brought about by the current evangelical awakening in America and elsewhere in all the historic Protestant denominations.

CHAPTER FIFTEEN

THE EVIDENCE OF FILLING

IN THE world there are no personalities exactly alike. Neither have any two experiences of conversion been exactly alike. So it is with amazement that one hears the question: "What is the experience of the Filling of the Holy Spirit like?"

The Holy Spirit has been compared with fire, wind, water, and other natural elements, so it is possible to have an experience of the Spirit as consuming as a forest fire, as bending as a hurricane, or as gentle as a well of water bubbling up from the depths like a river glorious in its perfect peace.

The great purpose in the Filling of the Holy Spirit is power for service, hence *the great evidence in the Filling of the Holy Spirit is power in service*, power unmistakably of the Spirit and not purely physical or psychic power. When a man, who has been known to have been seeking an infilling, is noticed to have developed great power in convicting sinners of sin, righteousness and judgment, or of leading other believers into profound truth, or simply of glorifying Christ by prayer or praise, it should be conceded that God has answered his prayer for power.

But there are other evidences of infilling. The fruit of the Spirit is love, joy, peace, patience, kindness, goodness, faithfulness, meekness and self-control. The word *fruit* is a collective singular.

The nine fruit of the Spirit must not be thought of as nine differing items, such as an apple, a pear, a peach, an orange, and the like, but rather as a cluster of grapes on a single stem, for all nine fruit hang together, and not one without the other (Galatians 5:22).

When a Christian is filled with the Holy Spirit, his heart is full of love. He cannot help it. He is possessed of a love for God transcending anything he has hitherto known. And if his heart is full of love, it is likewise full of joy unspeakable, which has to be experienced to be appreciated. And if it is full of joy, it is full of peace that passes all understanding. These three fruit, love, joy, and peace, are primarily God-ward, though they produce the same attitudes man-ward.

If a man's heart is full of peace towards God, it is possessed of a profound patience towards his friends, neighbours and even enemies. Once he has lost his patience with people, he has lost his peace with God. And patience permits kindness, just as impatience provokes unkindness. And kindness gives way to real goodness. These three fruit are primarily man-ward, though of course they reflect the attitudes of God.

The last three, faithfulness, meekness, and self-control, are primarily self-ward, being effective in discipline, humility and temperance. Each of these three is related to the other, and all three are related to the other expressions of the nine fruit of the Spirit.

The fruit of the Spirit is the real and immediate test of *the abiding fullness of the Holy Spirit*. A couple of missionaries, locked up in jail like Paul and Silas, have not much evidence on hand to demonstrate power in soul-winning, but the fruit of the Spirit will enable them to sing praises at midnight, to remain in jail in order to reach a jailer, and to be ready in season and out of season with the gospel.

A man may be pleased to offer other evidence of his having had a great enduement of power from on high, such as a gift of prophecy or the gift of tongues. But the gifts and callings of God are without repentance, and a man may still be exercising an evangelistic or other gift after the power of the Spirit has departed from him. Not so with the fruit of the Spirit, which abides as long as the fullness remains. Impatience may rob a man of his peace, but a moment of prayer and penitence restores it.

The Apostle Paul, in the First Letter to the Corinthians,* lists nine gifts of the Spirit which are quite distinct in nature and number from the nine fruits. The nine gifts are: wisdom, knowledge, faith, healing, miracles, prophecy, discernment, tongues and interpretation.

These gifts of the Spirit are supernatural gifts, and must not be confused with natural talents. A Christian worker may be naturally talented in singing, but his voice was noted in his unconverted days in other than Christian worship. Another Christian may be gifted in public speaking, but his talent could have been used in political work as readily. The gifts of the Spirit are supernatural, and are manifestations of the power of the Holy Spirit in creating spiritual rather than physical or psychic talent.

The gift of wisdom is expressed in remarkable insights given to Spirit-filled men. It is wisdom far beyond and far different to human wisdom. The gift of knowledge seems to refer to accumulated knowledge of the ways of God as expressed in His

*12:4-11

Word or His leadings. Campbell Morgan was a man with the gift of knowledge of the English Bible, just as A. T. Robertson had a gift of knowledge of Koine Greek. The gift of faith is not merely an enlargement of the faith possessed by every Christian, but is a special gift for a special task, such as the faith of Hudson Taylor for evangelizing China, the faith of George Müller for his orphans, and the like. These three gifts appear to be inward expressions operative upon the recipient's own heart primarily.

The gift of healing is a gift with a benefit directly toward others. As one who believes in divine healing as well as the use of human therapy, just as Paul healed the sick but left his friend Epaphroditus ill at home, one can see the gift of healing at work both with ministers of the Gospel and with Christian medical men, who more and more recognize that there is a communication of healing power between physician and patient which is not mere prescription or medicines or treatment. Likewise, the gift of miracles is one of benefit towards others, for one never reads of anyone working a miracle for his own exclusive benefit. Prophecy is another gift with most immediate benefit towards others, for it consists in forth-telling the ready message of God to the people, leading to their conviction or conversion or restoration or renewal or infilling.

Prophecy is the greatest of the gifts given in the First Corinthian Letter, the one which the Apostle urges the believers to covet the most (1 Corinthians 14:1–5). Prophecy is the great evangelistic gift, and, in times of revival, the gift is seen at its best advantage in the great evangelists and revivalists.

Discernment, tongues and interpretations are mystery gifts. They cannot be analysed or explained. I knew of an English-speaking evangelist visiting Norway during the Revival of the middle 1930s, humanly baffled in leadership of meetings because of the language difficulty, turning to God to seek the promised discernment of the spirits of men, which discernment continued to operate in his ministry but only in meetings in which the Spirit of God was working. Tongues, as described in 1 Corinthians, appears to be a humanly unintelligible ecstatic utterance of the spirit speaking in mysteries to God, not the utterance in human language recorded at Pentecost. This gift of tongues is relegated by the Apostle Paul to a place of less desirability than the others, as one that is self-edifying, unintelligible to even the speaker unless interpreted, confusing to the outsider, prone to indulgence and leading to confusion unless safeguarded. Interpretation is the parallel gift whereby another Christian, with his human understanding still unenlightened, makes known to the congregation what has been said. As neither tongues nor interpretation appear to be rational, there is little use in trying to explain them to the human mind.

In my opinion, the greatest hindrance to the progress of spiritual gifts among Evangelical believers is the view that the filling of the Holy Spirit must *always* be accompanied by speaking in tongues. This is a doctrine inferred from debatable scriptures and certainly far from explicit in them, and yet it is preached and practised with greater vehemence than the non-controversial advocacy of the fruit of the Spirit.

The Holy Spirit apportions the gifts to each one individually as He wills, therefore to insist upon the gift of tongues is a presumption upon the prerogative of the Spirit of God. Advocates of the doctrine of the necessity of tongues have been forced to deduce a subsidiary doctrine of the "initial evidence of tongues" as something quite distinct from the "gift of tongues" just as some of them teach that the Spirit of God is quite distinct from the Spirit of Christ, a similarly artificial doctrine.*

The Apostle Paul urged the Corinthians not to forbid speaking in tongues, but to do it in decency and in order, and to covet the best gifts. That is good advice for today. The gift of tongues can be faked. A good friend of mine, a Pentecostal pastor, told me how he and another pastor born in Europe tested the discernment of a congregation in Los Angeles. In an open meeting, the Lord's Prayer was recited in French and the Beatitudes in Dutch, where upon an interpreter arose and gave an "interpretation" of the message, something wholly unrelated to its content. I have known cases where a godly pastor or leader recognised such faking, and sharply rebuked the conscious or unconscious faker. Why should anyone attempt to fake tongues? If nine young men were seeking to be filled with God's Spirit, but each one was determined to speak in tongues and to refuse another gift as the evidence, the obvious outcome would be nine young men, or possibly eight, still tarrying for their self-appointed evidence, trying every possible method of inducing the ecstatic utterance. Furthermore, as others of their friends have already spoken in tongues, genuine or otherwise, they feel that their continued lack of evidence is a reflection upon themselves. In despair, they are quite ready to try anything. I know of one young evangelist who was urged to make up tongues as he went along and accept by faith as tongues whatever he managed to utter! It cannot be gainsaid that non-Christian or non-evangelical groups have also demonstrated their tongues, which

*For example, 1 Peter 1:10-11 states, "The prophets...inquired what person or time was indicated by the Spirit of Christ within them"; cf. Nehemiah 9:30, "by thy Spirit through the prophets".

shows clearly that the glossolalia can be simulated. However, it is happy to note that the insistence upon tongues as the exclusive evidence is waning in direct proportion to the waxing of interest in real revival among all denominations.

What actually is the Filling of the Holy Spirit? The Apostle Paul tells us: "Do not get drunk with wine, for that is debauchery; but be filled with the Spirit" (Ephesians 5:18). In alcoholic intoxication, a man is possessed by an alien spirit: a quiet man becomes rowdy, a mean man becomes generous, a decent man becomes bestial, a cautious man becomes reckless: and folks excuse him by saying that he is not himself, he is intoxicated. The filling of the Holy Spirit is God-intoxication; not fanaticism, but the possession of a man's faculties by the *Holy* Spirit of God, whereby his acts resemble acts of a Divine Being, who possesses him. The fruit of the Spirit is the very opposite of extravagance or fanaticism.

An interested pastor told me in conversation that he was actually scared of being filled with the Holy Spirit. Why? He said that he was afraid of what he might do. Such as what? Acting in a strange or fanatical way! I told him that he was insulting Jesus Christ by accusing the Holy Spirit even indirectly of fanaticism. The Holy Spirit is referred to as the Spirit of Jesus, the Spirit of Christ. As Christ was the perfect gentleman in His earthly ministry, so the Spirit of Christ is the Spirit of all gentlemanliness. The pastor's remarks were as insulting to Christ as would be an observation by a pastor that he was afraid to invite an evangelist and his wife to stay in his home in case the wife wrecked all the furniture!

How, then, may one seek to receive the en-duement of power from on high? Christ told His disciples, in the quiet conference following their request that He teach them to pray: "If you then, who are evil, know how to give good gifts to your children, how much more will the heavenly Father give the Holy Spirit to those who ask Him?"

The receiving of the Holy Spirit in His indwelling residence is something which the believer receives automatically when he receives Christ as Saviour. One has never known of a case where an unregenerate man asked God to give him the indwelling of the Holy Spirit, but rather of instances where the sinner cried to God for forgiveness or mercy or salvation or life. The words of our Lord seem not to refer to regeneration, but to the enduement of power from on high, the infilling power of the Holy Spirit.

It is in this connection that Christ said: "Ask, and it will be given you; seek, and you will find; knock, and it will be opened to you." An asking, seeking, knocking Christian will soon find out for himself what stands in the way of the filling of his vessel with the Holy Spirit, the clean and righteous and convincing Spirit who hates sin and unrighteousness and compromise. The Holy Spirit will lead him to seek forgiveness of his shortcomings through the cleansing blood of Christ, and to accept by faith His provision for a victorious life, fully surrendering himself to God. Then, by faith, and only by faith, the seeker may act upon the promises of God and receive into his most unworthy vessel the mighty power of the Spirit.

CHAPTER SIXTEEN

PERSONAL WITNESS

I HAVE hesitated a long time over writing a concluding chapter in a personal strain, but, after
much prayer and definite leading, I feel that I
ought to conclude this treatise on Full Surrender
with personal testimony—for two reasons: first, it
is not considered improper for a man to tell others
of the way of salvation and then add his own
testimony; second, there is not much persuasion in
writing chapters on the surrendered life if one has
no testimony to offer thereon. This said, I will not
offer any apology for personal reference, and will
content myself by praying that the testimony may
give all the credit to the Heavenly Father who gives
good gifts to His children.

My mother, youngest daughter of a family
brought up in the country district where the Irish
Revival of 1859 first appeared, led me to Christ
when I was a boy of nine, on my ninth birthday.
She held the theory that a child's heart takes
impressions like wax but keeps them like marble:
so she believed that no child was really too young to
trust the Lord for salvation. I honour her memory
for this.

Until I entered the College of Technology in
Belfast at the age of thirteen, I was a consistent
Christian insofar as small boys can be consistent.
But at the Tech., whose courses carried me as far
as London Matriculation (or Junior College level

in America), few of my friends knew that I was a Christian. I did not swear or drink or commit any of the grosser sins, but neither did I attend prayer meetings or evangelistic services except as a family duty in the company of my mother or brothers and sister.

About the age of seventeen, I began voluntarily to take an interest in spiritual things, and, never having been baptised, I sought baptism in the church of our family loyalty, Great Victoria Street Baptist Church, the downtown church of the denomination in Belfast, of which my second cousin by marriage, David Henderson, was pastor. When my father died in 1922 and left us as orphans without support, this church showed its consideration in a way that made me regard it all the more as the church of my childhood.

Shortly afterwards, through interest in a girl friend, I began to attend the Tuesday Christian Endeavour meetings in Cregagh Methodist Church. That was the Lord's way of introducing me to Christian ministry. Then the writings of Mrs. Howard Taylor began to fascinate me, and I became interested in the work of the China Inland Mission.

These were the various spiritual factors in my life when the Lord gave me the call to preach, which I first obeyed in open-air ministry in 1932, when I had turned twenty. I became busy in the great Belfast Youth Evangelistic Campaign organized by Christian Endeavour and the churches that year, and more and more I got interested in the literature of the great religious revivals of the past. As a result of this, my friends and I, all young men, formed the Revival Fellowship to pray for spiritual awakening around the world. We decided, wisely I think, not to make it a formal organization but to keep it a loose fellowship.

Up to that time, I had much to be thankful for in my Christian life, but there were also grave inconsistencies in my private life, which brought me more and more to the place of despair so graphically pictured by the Apostle Paul in the seventh chapter of Romans. In August 1933, when our Fellowship was at its peak in Ulster, I was in despair over my need of a deeper Christian experience.

I turned to a friend whom I regarded as more spiritual than myself, Charles Coulter, who knew how to pray. Like me, he was puzzled over the conflicting teachings of various groups about Sanctification and the Holy Spirit, but he was more definite in his views than I, for he had a Salvationist background. I was most uncertain about the things in my mind, but in my heart I was convinced that the Lord who had provided deliverance from the guilt of sin must have made provision for the hunger of His child for victory over the power of sin.

One Monday night, the 14th day of August, Charles Coulter and I made an appointment with a young Englishman serving a Belfast Church, Rudkin by name. Pastor Rudkin gladly gave up his evening off to discuss the deeper life with two young Irishmen, and, after two hours, at ten o'clock in the evening, my mental grasp of the way of full surrender was almost as clear as my heart's hunger for it. I differed with Rudkin on terminology, but I did not care much about mere words, and the Lord could read my heart and his.

As the clock struck ten, Pastor Morgan, his senior colleague, entered the drawing room to suggest tactfully the adjournment of the discussion. I was just then asking Rudkin: "Then what hinders me becoming surrendered and filled for service?" We knelt to pray.

It was the first occasion in my life when I felt in my heart that God was talking to me. It was not with a voice outside my ears, but through the indwelling Holy Spirit. I remember praying and assuring the Lord that I was willing to do anything, anything to be surrendered and filled. Then the others prayed in turn, but I have no recollection of what they said. The inner Voice said: "What about your besetting sins?"

My besetting sins? I hated them, loathed them, confessed them, vowed to have done with them. I considered them comparatively no problem, for I knew that the Blood of Jesus Christ cleanses the sins confessed to Him. Then said the Voice: "What about your will?"

That was an entirely new thought to me. I reflected that I was taking correspondence courses with the China Inland Mission with a view to becoming a candidate as soon as my mother was provided for; so I told the Lord in prayer that I was willing to become a missionary anywhere, or to stay at home, or to go into the ministry, or to stay in business. I felt rather pleased with myself that I was so willing.

Then the Spirit of God spoke to me about an idol in my life, a love affair, and asked me whether or not I was prepared to give it up if God so required. I suddenly realized that I was not willing, but I tried to pretend that I was. In other words, I was willing to do anything for God provided I had my own way in the love affair mentioned.

In case someone may feel that this was a lot of unnecessary fuss over an adolescent love affair, the following story may illustrate the importance of petty things. A young businessman received an urgent phone call from his wife, and came home by taxi, expecting the worst about his six-year-old boy. Sure enough, the doctor's car was at the door, but it was not so tragic as anticipated. Little Johnny had put his little fist inside a precious Chinese vase, and could not get it out without smashing the work of art. The mother and the doctor wanted permission from the father to break the vase. Not on any account, said the exasperated father, protesting how much he had paid for the vase. But cold water and olive oil and all other methods failed to permit Johnny to withdraw his hand, so, as the mother pointed out that their beloved child could not be expected to go through life with a vase on his hand, the father gave a reluctant assent to the use of a hammer. It was at that point that young Johnny asked if it would help matters were he to drop his penny. The little rascal had been willing to let his parents smash a work of beauty in order that he might keep his grubby little fist around a miserable little penny which had been dropped within the vase!

I too was willing to let my Heavenly Father smash the vessel He had prepared for my life in order to keep my fist shut tight on an adolescent token of love. I was just as determined not to let go; so I argued. The Spirit of God left off speaking within my heart, and my heart grew cold, so cold that I was frightened. So, my hunger for more of God returning, I let go, and cried to God for blessing, surrendering my will concerning the remaining unsurrendered area of my life. I accepted the blessing by faith.

I would no more think of describing in detail the spiritual experience which followed than a man would think of describing his honeymoon to strangers. I can say that my heart was flooded with love, joy and peace unspeakable, too great to bear. This was noticed by my friends, whom I had forgotten. The prayer meeting closed at two in the morning. For the first time in my life I felt that I really knew my God and Saviour, that Christianity was not merely a teaching or belief or philosophy. I felt the impact in mind, will and heart. The memory of that hour is always precious to me.

With a light step I walked home. Walking was not the word, for I ran down one street like a man with a telegram of good news. At three in the morning, I was kneeling by the rocking chair in the kitchen, trying to pray quietly so that my light-sleeping mother upstairs would not hear me. Then the sunshine was interrupted by a cloud, for the Lord reminded me of petty sums of money I had stolen from my mother's purse seven years before. I promised to confess it, and then I found that I was still walking in the light.

Next morning Mother asked me what time I had come home the previous night. Normally I would have equivocated by fifty-five minutes, and I felt like keeping silence so as to avoid discussing intimate spiritual matters with one of my own family, a thing always difficult to me. Upon reflection, I decided that if my experience was real, I had nothing to hide: so I told her briefly why Coulter and I stayed up late. I waited for the anticipated parental lecture on her pious hopes for an improvement in my behaviour at home.

Instead, I found that my mother seemed upset. It appeared that she had waited behind in a Faith Mission meeting seeking full surrender and the filling of the Holy Spirit more than twenty-one years before. She had been disappointed that God did not call her to extraordinary service after that, but she comforted herself in her monotonous household tasks by hoping that the Lord would claim the unborn baby within her at that time.

The following month, circumstances confirmed a leading to start out with only half a crown (half a dollar) or so, to go around the world as a messenger to the whole Christian world, urging believers everywhere to pray and prepare for a worldwide awakening. Within a month, my girl-friend terminated our friendship without suggestion from me. Thus began the early stage of my ministry, when for two years I was an apprentice in the life of faith, living from hand to mouth, travelling from Land's End to John o' Groats in the British Isles, and from Gibraltar to Moscow, from Oslo to Jerusalem. I told the story in three travel books whose last chapters indicate the message and experience of those days —*Full Surrender, Prayer and the Coming Revival, Hindrances to Revival, The Price of Revival, The Filling of the Holy Spirit.*

The second stage of my ministry began in September 1935, when I left for a world tour of the British Dominions and the United States of America. In odd places, occasionally, in Canada and the States, I saw local revivals of great intensity, the fruits of which abide to this day, as others will testify. The same was true in an increasing degree in New Zealand, Australia and South Africa. Ninety per cent of the ministry was directed to Christians, and ninety per cent of the results occurred among believers, nevertheless there were approximately ten thousand *professed* decisions of inquirers seeking salvation in that single year. Regarding the abiding results in conversions, I would not think of claiming that the ten thousand recorded decisions stood, but encounters with converts in missionfield, ministry, lay witness and other fields of Christian service lead me to think that the proportion of perseverance was not less than that of popular evangelism in this country. However, the ministry was mainly to Christians on Spiritual Revival.

At the end of this period, I had utterly no guidance as to the future. I went off to Lapland to pray, but the only clear guidance I received was concerning marriage, as a result of which I entered married happiness not surpassed by anyone known to me.

Then came a time of eclipse. In my own strength, I set out systematically to become a great evangelist, and took a team to Australia, where Chapman and Torrey achieved their start. Perhaps a thousand decisions for Christ were made, but there was less blessing in the six months with seven workers than there had been in the earlier six weeks alone. I afterwards discovered that there had been grave scandal in the lives of a couple of the workers, but the less said about that the better.

During this time, I neglected the ministry to which God had called me—Revival, collective and individual—and concentrated on direct evangelism. I can only say in retrospect that the Lord was not with me in power; neither was I conscious of any grave disobedience in my life. But the warmth of interest in the work of the Spirit in reviving the Church and quickening believers certainly declined. This continued for a couple of years, during which I had limited blessing by repeating the tactics and ministry of earlier days, but without their power.

In 1940, I felt decided to go back to school. The purpose of the five years of study may be gauged by the topics of the Th.D. dissertation at Northern and the D.Phil. thesis at Oxford, histories of the great awakenings of 1858 in America and 1859 in Britain respectively. These pursuits were interrupted by three years or so of military service as an Air Force Chaplain in the Pacific War, in which the Lord greatly blessed evidential evangelism among college and high-school graduates who came under my ministry. This was not revival, but very blessed military evangelism.

During the years of dearth, I made the acquaintance of a remarkable man of God of my own age. In America, I knew two people whose burden for Spiritual Awakening of the historic type was as great as my own at its best: Mrs. Henry M. Woods of the Worldwide Revival Prayer Movement, and Dr. Ernest W. Wadsworth of the Great Commission Prayer League. For reasons unknown to me, Mrs. Woods never seemed to respond to any friendly advances I made, and I lost contact with Dr. Wadsworth. But God raised me up a friend who never ceased to remind me of my original call, Armin Richard Gesswein, a Lutheran pastor who started writing to me about the prospects of revival as early as 1937, who saw real revival in Norway that year, and who never ceased to talk about it to me, often causing me to rake the embers of interest in revival and the deeper life.

During my Oxford studies, the interest in worldwide revival grew in my heart as I read the stories of God's wondrous doings in the past. Young American evangelists, knowing that I was in Oxford, began to make pilgrimages to my home in Wolvercote. I talked to them all about revival. Among them were several men who spent a day talking more about the hope of revival in this modern age than about anything else. I began to pray that if the Lord did not intend to use me further apart from writing the message, He would use me to pass on the burden to younger men. I developed a great affection and burden for one or more who afterwards became prominent in the 1949 Awakening.

One day, in London, in 1948, I sat listening to a saintly man of God, Andrew MacBeath, secretary of the Keswick Convention. He told a striking story of a visitor to France who used to pray in the quiet of a little French Roman Catholic parish church. The British visitor noticed that a middle-aged French lady used to come each morning regularly, make the rounds of the Stations of the Cross, and then spend half an hour in rapt adoration of a beautiful picture of the Virgin Mary. The visitor commented on her devotion, but the parish priest reluctantly told him that, thirty years before, the lady had posed for a Parisian artist's picture of the Virgin, and that she was really only contemplating the beauty she once was herself.

That story stung me, for then I dearly loved to contemplate the days when I had been getting attention as a worldwide evangelist in 1935 and 1936. The upshot of it was that I began to pray that God would give me something to be grateful for in 1949. The burden returned, not only for revival, but for the Filling of the Spirit.

Before 1949 began, Gesswein and I teamed up in a Ministers' Conference in Minneapolis and there saw an outpouring of the Holy Spirit, the first page in a new chapter, the current awakening among ministers throughout America. In March 1949, we shared ministry again in a greater conference of ministers, four hundred ministers and missionaries and evangelists and leaders and their wives meeting for protracted prayer meetings for revival in Los Angeles, and again we saw a greater outpouring of the Spirit, the turning point in the Awakening in California.

In April 1949 it was my privilege to see the first outbreak of revival on a college campus in the current movement, that at Bethel College in St. Paul, where a happy combination of evidential evangelism, narration of revival history and deeper life teaching was honoured of the Lord. I returned to my original call to preach the means of Awakening and the way of Full Surrender. The college awakenings continued. An evangelist and I shared midnight prayer about the Bethel meetings before they began, and he was impressed when the break came. His own faith in revival was being developed.

It was at Forest Home Conference Grounds in the beautiful San Bernardino Mountains of California that I shared ministry with my evangelist friend again, who daily consulted me about the topics of the talks, which were the topics of this treatise. I discovered something encouraging. The conversation of evangelists, like that of other professional people, is very much a comparing of notes or discussing of incidents peculiar to the life of evangelists. But in discussing historical revival and the deeper life, this consecrated and widely travelled young man was altogether an eager inquirer or listener. I think that the climax was reached after midnight one Wednesday night, when he opened his heart and told me of his desire for a renewal of his consecration and an anointing of the Holy Spirit.

At two in the morning, he returned to my cabin to tell me that he had received not only the sought-for blessing but an assurance that he was going to see real revival in his forthcoming campaign. Little did I know what was to follow, but I did learn that his ministry began to change from good to better. I heard this evangelist preach to many thousands on the Filling of the Holy Spirit, a hitherto untouched subject, and, more remarkable still, preach the same sermon twice in the same campaign. I saw God answer prayer for a willing evangelist.

Since that time, I have sought out evangelists, especially young men, and talked to them fraternally about the enduement of power from on high. I have scarcely ever known one to be indifferent. Some have talked until two or three in the morning, and I have been surprised myself to find such a burden for one and another that I have continued in prayer until dawn for them. All of them asked for the details of the message, scriptural references, and the like, until I came to the point that I felt that if, humanly speaking, I had only a month to live, I would spend it writing down my message.

The message is simple. Our wonderful Saviour not only made provision that His children by faith might be delivered from the guilt of sin, but He also provided a clearly-stated way whereby the shortcomings of His children might be confessed and forgiven and cleansed at any time. His Word also teaches that the obedient Christian by faith may claim victory over sin, enter into a closer walk with God, fully surrender his life, and be filled with the Holy Spirit of God for whatever service He may direct.

This is individual revival. Multiply it in faith, and there develops congregational revival, community revival, national revival and worldwide revival of Christians, with resultant soulwinning and missionary endeavour. There is a price to pay, but the reward is far greater.

This book is sent out, therefore, with the prayers of many as well as of the author that it may encourage the reviving of the Christian experience of pastors, evangelists, teachers, church members, new converts, and all whom the Lord may choose to bless.

It is my opinion that this devotional classic by the late Dr. J. Edwin Orr has been out of print and difficult to find for far too long. This edition of *Full Surrender* has been prepared and published with the approval of the family of Dr. Orr. This is a copy of the fourth edition.

God has spoken to many people (myself included) in a deep and meaningful way through this book, and I highly recommend it to you for individual devotions, group study, and personal reflection.

Dr. Orr's resources in audio, video, and text are available at:

www.jedwinorr.com

If you have questions or comments, you may send them to me.

David Guzik
david@enduringword.com

Printed in the USA
CPSIA information can be obtained
at www.ICGtesting.com
LVHW081452300124
770369LV00007B/113